Unwin Education Books: 36
LANGUAGE IN TEACHING AND LEARNING

Unwin Education Books

Series Editor: Ivor Morrish, BD, BA, Dip.Ed (London),
BA (Bristol)

Unwin Education Books: 36

Series Editor: Ivor Morrish

Language in Teaching and Learning

HAZEL FRANCIS
MA, PhD
Lecturer in Education, University of Leeds

London

GEORGE ALLEN & UNWIN

Boston   Sydney

First published in 1977

© George Allen & Unwin (Publishers) Ltd, 1977

ISBN 0 04 407003 9 cased
      0 04 407004 7 paperback

Photoset in 10 on 11 point English Times by
Red Lion Setters, Holborn, London.
Printed in Great Britain by Biddles Ltd, Guildford, Surrey

Preface

Why another book on language in education? Surely, after the spate of publication in this field in the last decade, we all know the importance of language skills. We know how children fail in school when they are 'lost for words' or cannot read; we know which children are at risk; we know what they ought to be able to do; and we have ideas of what to do about it all. Or do we? Many teachers seem to be aware of recent work; but they may not have been able to pull it together, to realise the nature of assumptions and gaps in the literature, and to see how problems of language use relate to actual teaching and learning. In fact the literature has stemmed more from a socio-linguistic than a psychological approach. Teachers may also have sought prescriptive programmes, but these tend to focus on very young children or on those for whom English is a second language; and even for these they are often found wanting. How far is it appropriate to develop specific programmes?

This book grew out of a feeling of need to put together something of the rather extensive literature relating to language and education, and in particular to place in perspective some of the work on disadvantage. It is hoped that teachers and trainee teachers might find it helpful in treading the maze of publications and in setting their own thinking and practice against a broader canvas. In attempting a wide coverage, with a considered discussion, reference has been made to many studies. It would scarcely be fair not to let interested readers know where they might pursue particular points, and the reader who may find the peppering of the text with names and dates a little distracting is asked to bear it patiently.

No tips for teachers are offered; nor are rules about how to teach or what to get pupils to learn; but the book does attempt to analyse and illustrate the nature and use of language in such a way that some broad principles of the possible understandings and misunderstandings in the classroom are explored. It acknowledges frankly the difficulties of teaching and appreciates the problems of task complexity and personal involvement, but it also emphasises the concomitant personal responsibility of the teacher for deciding what to teach and how to set about it once certain broad constraints are satisfied. These are seen as matters to be worked out with pupils rather than ready-made rules that can make life easier. This being so, the teacher's need for support in his work is recognised, but discussion and morale boosting may be more helpful than mere advice. As a first school headteacher said recently in conversation about children's talking and reading skills, 'the more precise language programmes are so often not suited to our conditions. The books and programmes that really help are those that make our own thinking clearer and give us more confidence to try what seems to suit our children'. This book is intended to help in the latter direction.

The first chapter is devoted to working out ways language is implicated in learning and teaching, while the next two chapters explore the language skills children bring to the school at different ages and from different backgrounds. The fourth chapter analyses the place of language in guiding learning and thinking, while the fifth treats the language of the classroom, with its mixture of control and instruction. The sixth is given to the development and use of literacy, and the final chapter pulls threads together so that the effects of success and breakdown in communication can be considered. The teacher's problem is clear, for while genuine dialogue has so much to commend it how can it be developed in the classroom? Thirty into one won't go! Perhaps we should be very cautious about attributing lack of attainment to language deficiencies in the home or in the child when all is clearly not well in the state of education.

Acknowledgements

The author is grateful to the following for permission to reproduce copyright material which is used in chapter 5:

Routledge & Kegan Paul Ltd, for extracts from *Social Relations in a Secondary School* by David Hargreaves, © 1967; Prentice-Hall, Inc., Englewood Cliffs, New Jersey, USA for a short excerpt from *Teaching Disadvantaged Children in the Preschool* by Carl Bereiter and Siegfried Engelmann, © 1966, p. 105; George Allen & Unwin Ltd, for an extract from *Beyond Control?* by Paul Francis, © 1975; Penguin Books Ltd, for an extract from *The Language of Primary School Children* by Connie and Harold Rosen, © 1973; The Open University, Walton Hall, Milton Keynes, for an extract from *Intervening in the Learning Process* by D. Moseley and D. Hamblin, © 1972, and for an extract from Marion Blank's Appendix to *Deprivation and Disadvantage* by M. H. Moss, © 1973; and to The Ford Teaching Project for quoted material from a paper 'Informal talk—informal education' by Clem Adelman, 1973.

Contents

1

Communication and Education

In this book the term 'communication' in relation to education is used to include many ways of transmitting and receiving messages, not simply 'telling people things'. Moreover, it is not assumed that talking by either teacher or pupil necessarily leads to learning; for whether various uses of spoken or written language actually promote specifiable learning is a matter to be examined, not one to be taken for granted. While specifying learning raises questions about the desirability and determination of objectives, which will find mention in the following pages, it also raises questions about our views of the nature of the learning process. We may ask how well, and to what other ends, teachers and pupils communicate with each other about their goals and about forging effective means of attaining them.

In relation to selected aims we have for some time heard how poor attainment in school correlates with features of the child's home background. The Newsom Report (1963), the Plowden Report (1967) and major research reports by Douglas *et al.* (1964, 1968) and Davie *et al.* (1972) present a full picture. More recently, however, studies have been directed to questioning how these features relate to the actual process of learning, and much has been said about deficient communication skill in children from relatively deprived backgrounds. Deutsch (1967), Riley (1967) and Wyatt (1969) described such work in America, and some of our concern in this country has received impetus from the American findings. Bernstein and his colleagues, working in London, have taken the view that children from different sections of the community learn to use language in different ways, and that such learning leads to different responses to education in schools, thus contributing to differences in educational attainment (Bernstein, 1971). While treating these issues and examining the nature of deficit and difference, this book's argument will take them to be only a part of the picture of the relationship between language and educational attainment.

In order to establish the outlines of this picture we can consider first the one-to-one teacher-pupil interaction. Many of us will think of relatively rare occasions within school, or of the engagement of a private tutor. But we do well to reflect on other possibilities, for in the ordinary encounters of everyday life we find children grasping new skills and ideas from a variety of individuals. Much early learning takes place in the daily

round of interplay between baby and mother, while later the youngster gains increasingly from the wider contact of the family circle and friends. The basic ways of thinking about life and of organising it in his culture are learned in these contexts, and the values and practices of adults are gradually comprehended. Except in areas heavily influenced by post-eighteenth-century European public educational practices, formal instruction of largish groups of children for long periods has been rare. Moreover, historical and anthropological accounts of 'institutionalised' instruction tend to show that it has been concerned more with training in specific skills or for particular roles than with education as we conceive it now. In choosing to educate our children in schools we tend to think of learning as confined to school, or to school-substitute situations; and then we fail to see how much one-to-one instruction goes on in a child's life—before he attends school, outside its walls during his school years, and in his subsequent apprenticeship into adult working life. When we impose an educational superstructure with a high teacher-pupil ratio on to this varied learning pattern and then speak of teachers acting *in loco parentis* we are doing something very odd; and the evaluation of what we are doing can be considerably illumined by analysis of the power and effectiveness of individualised instruction.

If a joint enterprise is to be successful to any extent some measure of agreement about goals is necessary. This implies that the parties are able to comprehend them and to understand each other's ways of talking about them. In an instructional context agreement is not easily obtained, especially when the learner is a child and power and initiative tend to lie with the tutor. This is markedly so in formal instruction when the aims may be determined by whoever is paying for it and are not negotiated with the pupil and perhaps not even with the teacher. For the child, learning may then become a mere duty rather than a sensible undertaking; and we can find in many an autobiography an account of a pupil's unwillingness to give more than a token acceptance of his lessons. Coaching of private pupils and the personal tuition often given by music teachers meet a similar lack of co-operation in some pupils, and perhaps in all from time to time. Yet, although the pupil may be little or not at all involved in the initial agreement, it can be quite possible for him to forge with the tutor some idea of what is to be done so that he feels involved and committed to the task. Lack of initial involvement is much less often found in the instructional exchanges of everyday life at home and in the world outside, but even there goals are not always as clear to the child at the beginning as they become during his learning. The lad who follows his father into the fields cannot conceive what it means to become a competent cultivator, just as the young violinist does not know what it will be like to be able to play really well. The quality of any instruction and learning will depend very much on the ways teacher and taught communicate with each other about the goals as the learning progresses, and some goals are easier to talk about than others. The end product of a training in some skill or role is more easily identifiable, even if not fully comprehended, than is the hoped-for outcome of an 'education'.

Effective instruction does not depend only on goal sharing, but also on agreement about the means of attaining ends. As in the case of goals, such agreement may be more implicit than explicit, but two people working together usually know whether or not they are in harmony. Not all tutors are able or willing to attempt to work for continuous co-operative endeavour with a pupil, many preferring to invoke the authority of their superior knowledge, or the power of their allotted position, to impose their own choice of the means of instruction, whether or not the pupil finds it useful. While a very conforming or obliging learner might accept such an imposition, many have personalities or attitudes that prevent full acceptance and their objections may interfere with their learning. Although in some circumstances their independence may be viewed as more valuable than the lost learning opportunity, the situation can only be viewed as a communication failure. Ideally, both tutor and pupil will engage in a continuing process of discovering and devising acceptable and appropriate means of learning, and this requires that they communicate adequately on this level. Possibly any deficit in the pupil's language experience will make for difficulty; but so will the teacher's failure to make himself clear, whatever the pupil's competence, and his failure to take up the ways in which the pupil sees the task. Can we suggest that teachers may sometimes lack language experience in relation to children as persons and learners?

As worked out in practice, the instructional process varies considerably. At one extreme of a pattern of interaction the tutor may adopt the strategy of presenting information to the learner on the assumption that if no learning takes place it is the fault of the pupil. Even with this limited approach he may still trouble at the end of his teaching to assess the nature and extent of learning—to obtain some terminal feedback. On the other hand he may simply leave the outcome unchecked. He is not then in a position to know how effective his teaching has been, but while the outcome might be negligible with one pupil it could amount to quite considerable learning with another. Without checking on what is happening the teacher can scarcely know what to do next and must teach in a quite arbitrary fashion. For this reason more frequent, ongoing checks on learning are often sought from the pupil in the form of questioning and testing. This alters the balance of communication between teacher and taught, a balance that can be shifted further by exploring the ways in which the pupil has incorporated new learning into his knowledge of the world or has failed to grasp it. In this situation the pupil is required not only to repeat or recognise what has been taught, but also to give an account of his interpretation of it. He must say much more. An even richer situation arises when the pupil spontaneously informs the teacher of his problems and asks for advice, information or guidance, while the optimal interaction includes the learner's contribution of additional relevant skills, information, interpretation, questions and problem solutions. It is possible in mathematics, for instance, for the pupil to produce a more elegant solution than the one the tutor had in mind. It is also possible in any topic for the pupil to construct a different and perhaps tutor-critical perspective. In such a situation teacher and pupil have become a problem-solving pair, recognising that two heads may be better than one.

It is now clear that effective instruction requires more than agreement as to ends and means, and more than the rich and complex exchange of information we have just sketched. It requires the sensitive use of language necessary to forge shared understanding of the nature of each other's knowledge and of the means of expression. Inevitably, since the processes of thought are ultimately private, complete mutual comprehension is never attainable; but some degree of publicly shared agreement can be worked out. Some of the most vital early learning of the infant is based on the increasing amount of shared meaning in action and in speech achieved by mother and child. The child's own knowledge of the world is modified and shaped in his contacts with his mother, while his language learning rests on the establishment of shared constructions of reality—however imperfect these may be. In this light, the concept of knowledge to be acquired that we must introduce into our discussion of learning cannot simply be one of something to be received like a package; it is, rather, a construction or series of constructions put by the individual on his experience. The relation between mental construction and verbal expression is unique to the individual. Two people using the same expression may construe it differently or, in the same situation, may use different expressions. One important feature of this view of knowledge is that shared understanding has to be seen as the interweaving, through verbal expression, of separate and unique systems of constructions. This applies even if a particular learning experience appears to be satisfactorily described for certain purposes in terms of a conditioning process or of rote learning. In these cases understanding and verbal expression are under-emphasised or minimised, but in most human learning the weight placed on verbal expression is very heavy. A delicate appreciation of each other's knowledge and language will facilitate the teacher-learner dialogue, but the task of leading another towards an insight on some issue cannot be guaranteed.

'A teacher cannot undertake to make a pupil understand. All he can do is present the sensible elements in the issue in a suggestive order and with a proper distribution of emphasis. It is up to the pupils themselves to reach understanding, and they do so in varying measures of ease and rapidity. Some get to the point before the teacher can finish his exposition.' (Lonergan, 1968, p. 5)

A person's knowledge then is the system of constructions he has put upon his experience, and his learning is the modification of this knowledge in the light of new encounters and new considerations. A session with a tutor is just one kind of new encounter introducing new possible considerations, but while the outcome will depend in part on the success of the participants in understanding each other's position and skill it will also depend on the appropriateness of attempted communication strategies in relation to what is to be learned.

Lonergan makes the point that while learning cannot be guaranteed it can be guided. He emphasises the selection, ordering and stressing of relevant elements, thus indicating that the teacher's role requires considerable judgement in relation to the pupil and the learning. This can be exacting and is often best done in an intuitive fashion by someone who has come to know both the pupil and the skill or knowledge well. It is the essence of teaching and is an art to be cultivated, drawing on whatever forms of communication seem most appropriate. It is likely that in training for what is predominantly a perceptual-motor skill, such as swimming or stroke play in tennis, proportionately more non-verbal communication will be consciously used than in a more purely cognitive task such as the understanding of selected historical events. In the former tasks physical example and physical guidance are found to be very useful, though the use of drama could add to the latter. Again, non-verbal aids like pictures and diagrams can be used in the learning of various craft skills and in the attainment of concepts in different areas of knowledge. Whatever the medium, the art of teaching is to use it in such a way that the intended message is maximally clear for the pupil concerned. Since much of a community's wisdom is recorded in written form, it is very important that both teacher and taught are conversant with written language in its many varieties. In order to be able to explore written material together both need to relate it to their own knowledge, and to learn how they each relate it to their own spoken forms of expression. This is as true for the youngster learning to read as for the sixth-form student of literature.

What our discussion so far means for teacher and pupil can be partly perceived by comparing the positions of two pupils, hitherto exposed to the knowledge and skills of a particular teacher, when one remains with his tutor while the other finds a new one. The pupil who remains shares with his teacher a history of tutorial sessions when, whatever unique patterns of constructions were formed, a considerable amount of shared meaning was established and ways of understanding each other's ways of communicating were worked out. For the pupil and teacher who are new to each other, however, there has been no such sharing, and understanding is still to be forged. In the process of new learning more assumptions about prior knowledge need checking if optimal understanding is to be achieved. It would be foolish, for example, to discuss calorimetry without ascertaining the nature of the pupil's existing concepts of heat and temperature in order to enable him to build upon them in such a way that the discussion is sensible. Equally, if unexpectedly pressed by the pupil whose knowledge is greater than the tutor anticipated, it would be foolish of the latter to undertake such an enterprise without being careful to examine his own understanding of the concepts, both in everyday use and in relation to scientific meanings. Further, it would be foolish to try to use forms of expression that were not familiar to the pupil, for that would be to embed the novel in the unknown. Obviously, much more work is demanded in starting a fresh tutorial relationship than in continuing an established one, which is not to say that it is detrimental to learning, but rather that it is more exacting.

The discussion so far has focused on knowledge as personally constructed; but it is also personally valued, and effective communication requires that attention be paid to value systems. The knowledge offered to the pupil is very varied. Some will be rooted in the values and experience of the teacher but most will be a selection of intelligent and artistic works by representatives of communities which have valued them in some other time or place. Kuhn (1970) has made this clear in relation to scientific knowledge and activity, but a little thought will suffice to allow us to conclude that the same is true of the work of artists, musicians, writers, historians and linguists, to mention only some of the fields of interest likely to be encountered by the pupil. And it soon becomes apparent that within these 'knowledge communities' subgroups make their own particular mark, valuing different aspects and uses of knowledge. Within established traditions of teaching, the question of which knowledge communities the child is being introduced to is rarely asked. But it is often asked about the new and the unorthodox, and is now increasingly asked within attempts to design new curricula. It should always be asked, however, if the pupil is to encounter new knowledge in a satisfying and satisfactory way, for it is intimately related to establishing the goals of learning. Recent considerations by sociologists such as Musgrove (1968) and Young (1971) are also bringing this kind of question to the fore, but perhaps somewhat confusingly, since the frame of reference is more often the nature of socio-economic groupings than the nature of knowledge communities. The two are not congruent.

In the actual learning process both teacher's and pupil's values will find expression. The teacher is more inclined to teach that which he values strongly in ways that he feels best. The pupil learns best that which he feels is worth learning, whether it be in relation to his own interests, his anticipated future activities, or the views of those persons he respects or admires. If the teacher figures as one of these then his values will carry weight more easily. Whether teacher and pupil make their views explicit verbally or whether they convey them non-verbally, they are likely to have some impact. Perhaps it is more important to consider non-verbal communication in relation to the valuing aspect of knowledge than to any other, if only because we tend to have less conscious control of this form of expression. What does the pupil make of the way the tutor handles books, or art forms, or scientific or musical instruments? What does the tutor's look and posture say of his attitudes to both the learner and what is to be learned? And what is the pupil saying silently of his teacher or of his learning? A reading of Argyle (1969) and Goffman (1959) will introduce one to ways in which these questions might be approached, while Pride and Holmes (1972) have edited a useful book to aid our understanding of the varied messages transmitted wittingly and otherwise in verbal encounter.

In general one can see that in teaching and presenting something of his personal stand in relation to the content of learning, the teacher can scarcely help conveying his views about the pupil, his performance, and possibly other aspects of his life than his learning. He comments verbally and non-verbally on the pupil's behaviour. He reacts to the pupil's appearance, manner, voice and many other traits in ways which are consistent with his preconceptions and expectations of the student. These may be fairly flexible, but they are often very stereotyped. Similarly, the pupil reacts to the tutor and effectively, though with less licence, conveys what he thinks and how he feels. These interpersonal exchanges can positively aid learning but they can also severely interfere with it, either through direct discouragement or through the confusion that reigns when the receiver misinterprets the sender's message. A mild illustration might be the pupil's understanding of *very fair* as *fair-to-poor* compared with the tutor's meaning of *fair-to-good*. Or a teacher who is accustomed to being addressed as *Sir* might well upset a pupil in whose previous experience such a mode of address has never been used, but who is nevertheless well acquainted with implicit attitudes of respect. These examples serve to show that, in being concerned in communication about their major goals and tasks of learning, both teacher and pupil are also involved in attempts to clarify and define aspects of their relationship and, in particular, of their relative status and means of controlling each other's behaviour.

So far our framework for discussion of communication in instruction has been based on a model of a one-to-one relationship between teacher and taught, but the experience of anything like individual tuition within a formal system of education is relatively infrequent for any one child. Most children, most of the time, learn in groups or classes. An adequate framework for discussion must therefore include considerations of agreement as to aims and means, and of processes of interaction in learning, where at least several persons are involved. Two models are worthy of attention. In the first case let us take groups of up to about a dozen. These constitute what the social psychologist is prepared to consider a small group. A major feature of such groups is that they are small enough for joint agreement to be established and maintained about the groups' goals and the ways of achieving them. Values and attitudes can be shared and members are able to sink differences and pull together, albeit with greater or lesser degrees of willingness. The social satisfaction of shared enjoyment and the task satisfaction of shared achievement can be very rewarding and tend to perpetuate the life of the group. The breakdown of school classes into small groups for learning purposes can result in enjoyable and successful work if the pupils respond as functioning groups. If, however, any group fails to develop adequate cohesion it is likely that either all the children within it fail in some measure at the intended task, or that whatever learning takes place is developed independently. Now once this is seen to be the case with small groups it readily becomes apparent that in the second model, the school class, one has to cease talking of simple group interaction. Whenever the teacher plans to involve all his class in the same learning task he is working in a context where cohesion is most elusive. The most likely situation is that he obtains a limited measure of consent to his proposals, and that in addition to this the informal groups within his class establish their own agreements about what is to happen.

Whichever of the two social settings is functioning, the small group or the school class, the role of the teacher in the process of instruction may vary just as it did in the one-to-one model. He may choose to place himself outside the circle of pupils, standing apart and involving himself only from that stance, in an attitude of keeping order and delivering the goods. Provided that order is maintained this is an excellent position for the man who is concerned primarily with a show of his own authority and for the man who wishes to set up defences against involvement with his pupils' learning. But a different tutor might choose to try to step within the circle to achieve some balance between directing and sharing in learning. In practice it is very likely that the tutor's position is in fact largely delineated by the pupils, for their joint pressures on him, arising from their perceptions of the situation and of him in relation to their group goals and norms, are very powerful. It is possible, indeed, that one group might draw him towards them, while another might quite clearly keep him outside. How far teacher and taught will be able to develop a rich process of interaction in learning will depend largely on the possibilities of establishing shared goal-directed communication, feeding all involved. Most of us realise that the richer possibilities are not often realised in practice in schools.

Recent work in social psychology as applied to education, work such as that of Hargreaves (1967), Lacey (1970) and Nash (1973), illustrates the way classes usually contain their own informal groups of pupils, some sharing the aims and values of the teachers, while others are very antagonistic. Early in school life children respond differently to teachers and learning tasks, some becoming closely involved while others show bewilderment, indifference or opposition. Like-minded children tend to draw together and their groupings are reinforced only too often by the teachers' behaviour towards them. By the time they have reached the years of secondary or upper schooling some groups are expressing opposition by antagonism and aggression, and indifference by lack of attention and by truanting.

If children with different upbringings come to school with different habits and expectations about the use of both verbal and non-verbal forms of expression, then these differences will not be confined to learning tasks but will extend to all aspects of teacher-pupil interaction. They will be evident in the language of control, both amongst pupils and between teachers and pupils. They will be revealed in forms of address, request, command, explanation, agreement and so on, through all aspects of social interaction in school. Features of this interaction in turn have repercussions on learning. In Hargreaves's (1967) study a lad from a lower stream who had been transferred to an A stream is quoted as saying of his new fellow pupils, 'They speak different too. Things like foul language. They don't swear much in 4A.' And a teacher, reprimanding 4B, said, 'This is 4B. You wouldn't believe that this was next to the top class. Does B stand for blockheads?' Levels of attainment, like social background, carry with them sets of expectations and limitations that are reflected in the language directed at and about pupils. Is it surprising that most pupils in school not only learn something of the knowledge they are supposed to acquire, but also develop revised perceptions of themselves and others?

Care of recalcitrant pupils as they near school leaving age has been a matter for concern. It is often the case that there is a correlation between unwillingness in pupils, low attainment and social background. The ways in which such an association comes about are complex and obscure. Banks and Finlayson (1973) discuss certain relevant features of parental interest, control and expectation, while Keddie (1971) takes up the point that aspects of knowledge are valued differently by various sections of the community. Many teachers find that the under-attaining pupil often sees what he is required to learn as being almost, if not wholly, irrelevant to him. Sometimes it seems he does not even begin to comprehend what kind of knowledge is supposed to be open to him through schooling. In these cases the child may never have felt involved in a sensible learning task throughout his school life, which is not to say that his schooling was unsuitable but rather that lack of basic communication about learning made it ineffective. This kind of failure reminds us that when we consider numbers of children from different background pools of experience we really begin to face some of the problems of trying to provide a universal system of education. Attempts to cater for mixed abilities are not enough; we must cater for a complex population, for an assortment of children in any one school who come from different communities with different forms of knowledge, different views of their needs in life, different values and aspirations, and different ways of expressing all these. Handicaps in learning do not stem only from different abilities and command of speech. Communication can break down for a variety of reasons.

To sum up the analysis attempted in this chapter we first emphasise that the teaching-learning process varies considerably with the persons and content concerned and with the communication strategies adopted. It is essentially a continued negotiation of ends and means, presenting the pitfalls of failure to agree and failure to co-operate, both of which may be due in part to failure to understand each other's forms of expression. Second, we emphasise that the process takes place between persons who bring to it prior relevant knowledge and skill, expectations of each other's communication competence, and perceptions of themselves and each other. For both teacher and pupil it ends, if anything has been learned, with newly constructed or modified skill and knowledge, with extended or revised communication skill, and with altered perceptions of the self and the other. This analysis can be applied to teaching children of any age or ability; and, while learning cannot be guaranteed in any encounter, ways in which it might be optimised can be considered.

This book explores what children can bring to the teaching-learning process as a consequence of their command of language and their previous learning, the possible uses of language in instruction, and how the actual process develops—pitfalls and all—in classroom contexts. Limiting the scope of the discussion to the activities of teachers and pupils as the central issue is a deliberate choice; but necessary references to the broader scene indicate something of the way language in school nests in the total picture of the formal provision of education and of the activities of the families for whose children it is devised. That more reference is made to the language, knowledge and values of the home and the pupils rather than to those of the educators is an imbalance that results in part from the state of educational theory and research in problems of educational attainment. It is an imbalance that provides food for thought.

2

On Language Development in the School Years

Bruner (1960) has claimed that any subject can be taught effectively 'in some intellectually honest form to any child at any stage of development'. Without taking up the challenge of exploring what might here be meant by 'effectively' and 'intellectually honest', it is at least possible to make the point that much will depend on how language is used in the endeavour. This will depend in part on children's capabilities in producing and understanding speech, and these will vary with stages of development. In this chapter we shall be concerned with a discussion of language development as a basis for effective instruction during the school years, bearing in mind that it is itself a product of learning and guidance.

It has been claimed that most 4-year-olds have mastered the essential grammar of their language, and, except that we may have sometimes encountered a severely handicapped or deprived child, we feel that there is much truth in this. Between two and four years most children show a dramatic change in their speech skills, moving from separately articulated 'words' to sequences of utterances that we can analyse as grammatical sentences and that serve a variety of the functions of speech. Summaries and discussion of research reporting the systematic nature of this development can be found in such work as that of Brown (1973) and Francis (1975), while an analysis of the functions of speech in early dialogue by Halliday (1973) sets the stage for an appreciation of the development of skill in communication. At some time in the first 3 or 4 years the possibilities of communication with persons other than those who have hitherto cared for them expand so much that it becomes possible and practicable to give young children nursery schooling as distinct from care. There is, however, substantial further language development during the school years.

Although at any age we may use very fragmentary or simple remarks that are embedded and interpreted in their context of use within the structure of gesture and event, older children and adults are more capable of abstracted or displaced speech than is the young nursery school child. Britton (1970) has described such speech as being related to other and more distant events than those in which the speaking occurs, and characteristic of reporting, narrating, discussing and explaining. It is usually more grammatically complete than active speech, bears interpretation without situational support, and is appropriate for more formal occasions. For the 3-year-old, however, even in a fairly formal interview situation when talking to a strange adult about some toys, only about half of the remarks can be described as grammatically complete (Templin, 1957). In most of his talking even the so-called complete remarks of the child of this age are open to misinterpretation by a stranger, for he is still very dependent on an understanding speech partner to extend the basic forms of speech and to learn their permitted use as practised by his elders. The tacit understanding built up between the mother and the growing baby is forced into greater explicitness as the child first crawls and then wanders further from his mother so that the focus of his attention cannot readily be perceived or directed by her. From the early functions of commanding attention and directing it to desired aspects of ongoing events, the child's language develops to refer to perceived objects and their attributes, relations and movements; to signal expectancies and report happenings; and eventually to recall past events and to plan future activities. From the immediate here and now the child extends his involvement into the distant, the past and the future, building his knowledge of language as he builds his knowledge of living.

Language ability can thus be thought of in many ways; but, assuming that the child is busy doing things with speech, we can see what sort of words and word patterns he commands at any stage. Let us first consider knowledge of words. If we sample the words used by a 3-year-old we are struck by the way it is possible to treat them like words in adult speech. Our interpretation of the child's use suggests to us that we can use descriptive terms such as noun, verb, adjective, adverb, and so on. To do so can be very useful as long as we are careful not to attribute some comparable grammatical knowledge to the child. At this stage new words may be acquired in several different ways. If one happens to be used in an otherwise familiar context, and if attention is focused on the relevant aspects of the situation, some kind of analogy may be made; and the child may then try out the new word for himself. The original user may be quite surprised to hear the word from the child, since he was not aware of being observed and had no intention of instructing. The acquisition of taboo words and expressions in this way forms the basis of many a parent's humorous or rueful tale; but what takes us by surprise in the case of such words is taken for granted in the case of much of what the child learns. A further basis for learning is to be told a word by another person who feels some need to use it in an interaction, and so to give examples of its use. Another way is to ask for help when frustrated in trying to express something. Natural language learning is a personal, social and thoughtful enterprise, much hedged about by mood and chance. Very rarely does the child outside school encounter the intentional instruction which is part of more formal education; and it may be true that even in school he learns more informally than formally.

The following is an illustration of spontaneous noun seeking by a child. *Mummy, There's a big long*, said the child, entranced by the sight of an aeroplane trail in the sky. One might have thought this odd, but the actual impression was of apt usage of the word *long*, no suitable noun being known. Then he said, *What's that?*, and on receiving the reply *An aeroplane trail* he repeated it slowly as though savouring it. Then, as the white vapour spread and turned a golden brown in the sunlight, he said, *Got brown sugar on it*, to which remark the mother replied, *Yes, it's like that, isn't it?* Now in this exchange there was much that was left unsaid. The child's grasp of the new expression was not tested (though he did use it appropriately shortly afterwards); and the nature of his thinking in the apparently metaphoric expression was not explored, though it was guided in the response. The child did not seem to think that the vapour really was brown sugar, but then he didn't know that it wasn't—nor did he know what the alternatives might be. A more instructional approach, aiming to teach the relevant vocabulary, might run the risk of tapping more uncertainty than certainty; and yet it could give the impression of limits and precision. The child might then be left with anxiety rather than curiosity, and the effort would appear ham-fisted and reductionist in comparison with the more incidental approach.

Most of the young child's nouns are concrete rather than abstract, but personal names and pronouns figure frequently in his speech. Pronoun use shows how different forms are needed according to function, for, while nouns, personal names and impersonal pronouns remain stable, personal pronouns shift and change in English. How does the child learn that *you* refers to himself as hearer, but to the other when he speaks? To make it more difficult consider a triad of Daddy, Mummy and son, Tommy. When Daddy speaks to Mummy, *Daddy = I, Mummy = you*, and *Tommy = he*; but when he speaks to Tommy, *Mummy = she* and *Tommy = you*. When Mummy speaks to Tommy, *Daddy = he* and *Tommy = you*. How does Tommy know that when he speaks to his parents he uses *you* to them and *I* of himself, and *he* of his father and *she* of his mother? To add to his problems, how does he learn to differentiate correctly between the case-marked versions *I/me, he/him*, and *she/her*? In one sense it would be correct to say that he learns by trial and error, since he obviously tries out his remarks with pronouns, and he makes such efforts as *Me going* and *Him not naughty*. But it would be a mistake to think that he learns by having his errors corrected, for most of the time such remarks are tolerated by parents in the expectation that the errors will vanish as the child grows. It might be more correct to say that he learns by trial and observation, if we regard the errors as by-products of the process rather than a basis for correction. How he comes to recognise the regularities and oddities of speech patterns and to conform to the norms is something of which we know very little, but between 3 and 5 years of age mo· children come to differentiate correctly most of the time; and where a local speech community uses forms different from standard English systematic dialect is learned.

Also between 3 and 5 years children learn to express plural forms of nouns and to adopt correct modifier use with both count and mass nouns. The pattern of learning seems to be very similar from child to child, though no two children follow exactly the same course. First a few examples of both regular and irregular forms are acquired; then some aspect of regular usage spreads across the board, sometimes being over-generalised. Perhaps other aspects also spread before irregularities are finally correctly redefined. Thus a child who began quite suddenly to use the voiced form of *s* as a plural marker for nouns ending in a voiced consonant or a vowel, whether he had met the noun before or not, also added the marker to *children* and *chessmen* in spite of previously correct use of both the singular and plural forms of these words. Later he reverted (or moved on) to the correct forms without altering his general rule. He also used *two cars* and two *coffees* (meaning two cups of coffee) until he mastered more number adjectives. Then for a short time he used phrases like *two coffee* and *six carriage*, but he soon revised this and adopted the plural noun form with all number adjectives. A moment's thought about the nature of the learning revealed by these 'errors' leads one to the realisation that simple overt correction of individual instances is not likely to aid the child much, and that there is a distinct possibility of either confusing or inhibiting him by repeated correction—even if such correction be no more than drawing attention to the 'error'. It would seem that what the child needs is an appropriate and varied model and time to sort out its intricacies. Some children will continue to make such 'errors' well into the school years. One 6-year-old was heard by the author to use *toofs tooken out* in an otherwise maturely expressed story.

This example leads us to look at other form classes as used in speech. Already by three years most children have acquired a useful stock of verbs related to the activities of everyday life—to eating, washing, dressing, movement, work and play. They can also talk of wanting and liking, of being able and being allowed to do things, of seeing and even of thinking and knowing. They then spend the pre-school years not only in acquiring further examples of verbs but also in developing the use of auxiliary and modal verbs. This is a rich field for potential 'error' as the regular and irregular forms of expression of tense and mood are worked out. It is in this context that vocabulary comes to include words such as *will, shall, won't, can, can't, must, should, would, could, might* and expressions such as *have to, got to*, and *had better*. Work undertaken by Shields and Steiner (1973) reports the developing use of such terms by children of pre-school age. It is the increasingly 'correct' elaboration of verbs and subject-verb agreement that plays a large part in leading us to judge that most children command the basic grammar of their language by four years or so. Moreover, the mastery of the use of these forms opens up much more differentiated and sensitive communication.

But speech that consisted solely of nouns, pronouns and verbs would be quite limited in scope. Both nouns and verbs are qualified relatively early in child speech. Between 3 and 5 years the development of the noun phrase shows a considerable use of demonstrative adjectives, of articles specifying whether the noun refers to a particular instance or to just one of many, and of adjectives which call attention to some identifying attribute of the person or object to which reference is made. Such adjectives imply use of the senses and of the hands in making judgements which yield descriptions of colour, size, feel and number; but they also include evaluative words such as *good, bad, naughty* and *pretty*. The verb phrase is elaborated by including adverbs such as *now, tomorrow, yesterday, there, here, fast* and *slowly*, verb particles such as *off, on, up* and *down*, and prepositional phrases indicating aspects of the time, place, purpose or manner of an event. The speech of the 5-year-old is thus likely to be relatively simple, quite basic in reference, and related to everyday activity; but it is nevertheless grammatically acceptable within the child's speech community and adequate for many purposes in a variety of contexts. Yet it is still very much embedded in, or held together by, the activities and thoughts of each individual child.

As adults we are able not only to group words into form classes but also to place them in semantic categories according to similarity in meaning. We can then compare children's groupings with ours. Again we need to be cautious about the nature of any organising skill we attribute to children, but we have some idea of what we are ourselves doing. We tend to group words commonly found in children's speech in the manner illustrated in Table 1. In doing so we are applying rules which work something like this. *Animal* is the name of a class of creatures of which *cat, mouse, dog* and *horse* are examples, but of which *robin* and *blackbird* are not. They are members of another class of creatures each of which is called a bird. But both animals and birds are animate, whereas *money* and *toys*, again class labels, are not. In the illustrated classifications some of the thinking is represented by bracketed category heads, but much is not made explicit. In the case of words like *more* and *on* similar classifications might be made in terms of number, space and time, but what is more obvious is that the words can be paired as poles of a continuum of some kind of measurable operation.

Now the question arises as to when children are able to do this sort of

Table 1

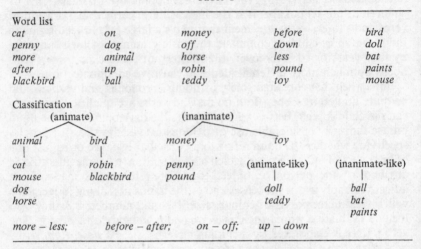

Word list

cat	on	money	before	bird
penny	dog	off	down	doll
more	animal	horse	less	bat
after	up	robin	pound	paints
blackbird	ball	teddy	toy	mouse

Classification

(animate)		(inanimate)	
animal	bird	money	toy
cat	robin	penny	(animate-like)	(inanimate-like)
mouse	blackbird	pound	doll	ball
dog			teddy	bat
horse				paints

more – less;   before – after;   on – off;   up – down

thing with words. The pre-school or nursery school child will often sort objects or pictures into classes, though with variable success since much depends on the complexity of the task, the bases of grouping and the child's ability to keep a basis in mind as long as is necessary. His play also reveals awareness in action of 'polar pairs'. But what of words? It is obvious that if we want an answer we cannot ask the child to try to do what we have done until he is able to read, nor can we give him the array of words orally and expect him to remember them. We couldn't even do that ourselves! We might, perhaps, break the task down, taking a few words at a time, so that we ask for something like the 'odd man out' in a group such as *toy, more*, and *doll*. Continued exploration might yield a classification system, but not all children below 7 years can perform such a task with words, and few would sustain it to the end. Even with those children who oblige us, we do not know the basis of their judgements unless we ask and receive a reply that we can take fairly confidently. It is not enough that a child groups as we do (even if that happens) for he may not be thinking about the words as we are. When children have been asked to make judgements of this kind they have compared words by noticing matching features or functions attributed to the referent objects (Lippman, 1971; Francis, 1972). They may pair *cat* and *mouse* because they are animals, but before 7 years they are more likely to do so because they both have tails, or because the cat chases the mouse. They are also just as likely to pair *little* and *mouse*, saying, *'You can have a little mouse'*. Indeed they can be extraordinarily adept at seeking relationships between the most unlikely pairs of words, not in terms of the semantic categories of adult thought, but in terms of the relations between aspects of imaginable events.

Another approach, usable with even younger children, suggests similar mental operations. Simple association tasks like *I'll say a word, then you say the first one you think of* yield more semantic class associations from adults and older children than from the younger ones. Some examples are given in Table 2, showing not only the general tendency but also something of the wider vocabulary choice of the adult and the marked tendency to react with antonyms from 7 years on.

Table 2

Word	Association				
	adult	11 yrs	9 yrs	7 yrs	5 yrs
table	statistics	chair	chair	chair	leg
man	woman	woman	woman	woman	arm
mountain	snow	hill	valley	hill	snow
dark	horse	light	light	bright	bed
deep	ocean	shallow	shallow	shallow	sea
soft	hard	hard	hard	hard	white

The young child's lack of such an inclination is more clearly understood after consideration of work which has set out to explore his responses to 'polar pairs'. Clark (1971) had children from 3 to 5 years act out instructions containing *before* and *after*. She found that the younger children tended to act *before* correctly and *after* incorrectly. Slightly older children reacted to *after* as if it meant *before*, but the 5-year-olds treated both correctly. Slobin (1966) reported some work by the Russian investigator Sokhin which tended to show a similar phenomenon with even younger children responding to *on* and *under*. Giving children of between 3 and 4 years instructions about hanging miniature apples on model trees, Donaldson and Balfour (1968) reported that they found the youngest children treating *more* correctly but *less* incorrectly, while at a later stage *less* seemed to be interpreted as *more*, and at 4 years both were beginning to be used correctly.

A first stage in the interpretation of these findings suggested that children were learning the adult semantic system, and that where they encountered terms with some dimensional reference they first realised the nature of the dimension and then began to mark it with the positive pole, only later differentiating the two poles and realising the need for a second word. But further work has made the picture clearer. Clark (1973) explored the possibility that the strategies adopted by children in their actions govern their responses to the words concerned. If, for example, a small child's inclination is to place one brick on top of another rather than to slide one beneath, then his response to a request to place any object on another is as likely to be a coincidence as a sign of comprehension, and we should not be surprised if there is a bias towards *on* rather than *under* in his apparent comprehension. Even when he is definitely associating the words with the vertical dimension (and this would have to be tested by contrasting such words as *on* and *by*), he would still have to find out that in our verbal expressions *x on y* is the same as *y under x*, but not the same as *x under y*. Small wonder that for a time he shows a bias towards treating *under* as *on*! In the case of *before* and *after* the instructions took the form of two-clause sentences, and it is possible that the children were not able to grasp the whole structure until they were 4 years old. A tendency to respond to the first clause first and not to notice the conjunction readily when it was in the middle of the sentence would lead to a bias towards more correct responses to *before* than to *after*. Donaldson and Balfour discussed several aspects of the problem of learning *more* and *less*, but one relevant strategy might be a tendency to treat taking an additional quantity of food or suchlike as more even if it were less than some implied amount. A child can have more orange squash even if it be less than the extra given to his friend, or less than what was offered to him. Admittedly these are no more than hypotheses, but Clark's suggestion that such strategies be explored may be a more useful approach to understanding children's use of language. More recent work by Donaldson and McGarrigle (1974) reports further uses of *all* and *more* by 3-5-year-olds in ways that are surprising to adults until the relevant strategies are explored. The children were comparing groups of toy cars in toy garages. When four cars filling four garages were compared with a group of three filling three, the former group was judged to contain more cars; but when a group of five garages containing four cars was compared with three full garages, then the latter, full group might be judged to contain more. Use of the word *more* related very much to the context in which a judgement was made.

In a further study by Clark and Garnica (1974) the verb pairs *come* and *go* and *bring* and *take* were examined, noting the dimension of approach/retreat in relation to the self as speaker. Here it was found that children of 5-9 had difficulty in sorting out the meaning of these verbs as used by two toy animals speaking to each other. The problem was not one of learning dictionary meanings, but of learning to shift a viewpoint from one speaker to another. In a different study Haviland and Clark (1973) found it necessary to consider strategies in an attempt to account for the pattern of learning of kinship terms. Attention to semantic features was not sufficient. They found, as Piaget (1928) and others have done, that a child may be able to say that he has a brother before he realises that he is also his brother's brother. Any adequate description of this state of affairs requires consideration of the child's psychological orientation; for to fully understand certain expressions of relationships he must be able imaginatively to stand in another's shoes, or in another place or time. The child under 9 cannot easily or always achieve such a shift of viewpoint, and his command of language reflects the fact that his construction of the world is not quite like the adult's.

Another aspect of shifting awareness is that which allows reflection on speech itself, rather than on the events of which it is a part. Britton (1970) has made the distinction between spectator and participant functions, the participant using speech in direct conversation relating to ongoing activities and the spectator reporting to someone about some other happenings. For example, taking part in a search John might suddenly exclaim, *There's the cave!*, This utterance would have a participant function. His companion, recounting the incident later, might say, *Then John said, 'There's the cave'*, making the remark from the stance of spectator at the original event and participant in the present exchange. Most nursery school children of 4 years or so can use speech in both ways, but there is a further level of spectator function which is found when the utterance itself is attended to. Thus John might also add, *That was exactly what he said*, indicating attention to the actual form and content of the remark. This kind of awareness is not often found developed in the young schoolchild. When, however, he can report and listen at some length, and observes his own reporting, then he gains an awareness of speech as a system which can be abstracted from the glue of events and reflected upon and used of itself. It may be that, as Vygotsky (1962) has suggested, it is crucial for success in reading that such an awareness be developed. We should not, however, attribute too sophisticated an awareness to the child, for it is not explicit and verbalised but is rather a 'gut' knowledge in the body of his perceptions and actions, and is one that comes from certain kinds of experience and insight.

As children approach 7 and are more able to hold in mind something they wish to tell at length, they are also able to produce more complex sentence constructions in their speech. Not that such forms are always necessary for the telling, but they do seem to be increasingly preferred, perhaps because more can be said in a given span with the more complex coding of meaning. Such coding has to be acquired, however, and possibly the best systematic linguistic descriptions of what is to be learned have been given within what is known as transformational grammar. Older descriptive schemes treat complex expressions as patterns of dependent and independent clauses, but do not describe their relations to equivalent simple sentence patterns. Although they do not entirely correspond, there is much agreement between the two approaches in terms of the sentence units on which analysis is based, and descriptions of children's speech based on the older approach still give useful indices of developing skill. Templin's (1957) measures of remark structure in a particular kind of interview speech showed a steady increase in the percentage of complex forms from 3 to 8 years of age. Isaacs (1930) reported the use of certain kinds of dependent clause patterns by children at the Malting House School in Cambridge. One has to make some allowance for the high intelligence of that particular sample of children, but noun clases such as *I don't know where it is* and clauses beginning with *because* were used by 4-year-olds, while relative clauses and those beginning with *if* were noticed at 5 years. In a story reproduction task the author (Francis, 1975) found some children of 5 saying things like *And when he had eaten all the biscuits he couldn't get off to sleep because there was not enough room for him, for the crumbs had gone all in his mother's pocket.* (The reference was to a small kangaroo.) At 7 some said things like *One day when Busybody was walking along, knitting in the street, she saw a boot hanging out of Teddy's window. She was so anxious to know why the boot was hanging there that she knocked at the door very, very loudly.* None of these sentences occurred like this in the model stories, though the content was expressed in a different form. At 7 years the frequency of occurrence of complex remarks of all kinds was greater than at 5, and this was true at all levels of ability. In this task children of 5 averaged 1.63 clauses per remark, while at 7 they averaged 1.86. Most clauses, though not all, were units corresponding to the independent and dependent clauses of traditional grammatical analyses. A simple sentence would therefore score as one unit, while a sentence with a main clause and one dependent clause would score two. That there was room for further development beyond 7 in that particular task was shown by the score for the stories themselves (2.34) and that for a group of young adults who were willing to retell the stories (2.37). What, we may ask, is the significance of this developing skill? It might best be summarised by saying that the ability to produce and fully understand complex sentences is the foundation of expression of complex relationships in observed events, of expression of logical thinking, and of definition of more abstract vocabulary items.

Let us consider the expression of complex ideas. It is important that we ask questions such as the following. If we ask *Why did the ice melt?* what difference is there between the answers *Because the sun warmed it* and *The sun warmed it?* And what difference lies between *The ice melted because the sun warmed it* and *The ice melted. The sun warmed it?* In both cases *because* is present in one expression and absent in the other. Its presence is usually taken to imply understanding of a causal relationship; though it is possible that the relation may be only partly or mistakenly comprehended, and the form may even be used as a kind of formula indicating learning of the approved mode in certain contexts without comprehension. Its absence raises further problems. Is *because* understood but not used because the speaker does not, either customarily or in this context, choose to use it? Or is its absence due to the speaker's lack of comprehension? The very juxtaposition of the two related ideas, however, suggests at least a partial comprehension. Let us acknowledge, then, that more elaborate forms of expression may convey no more, nor indicate greater understanding, than combinations of simple forms. Nevertheless, the bias in our usage is towards more elaborate forms with age and with more formal contexts. In formal instruction settings in school we tend to make relations explicit, and expect that appropriate complex expressions will be used. We also tend to judge chldren's verbal ability and comprehension in such a way that we infer more competence on both fronts from more elaborate and explicit expression.

We can err, however, if we assume that children understand such expressions as we do. The question of psychological abilities and strategies is as important in this respect as we saw it to be in our consideration of word meanings. Watts (1944) found the conjunctive *although* difficult for 7-year-olds, and even at 10 only about half of the instances of its use were correct in testing of appropriate use. Not until 15 were most children able to use it correctly. He also found that *because* and *If ... then* were only used correctly most of the time by children under 7 when applied to relations between clauses referring to sequential events of some personal relevance; but the same forms were not understood if applied to hypothetical relations or generalisations until children had reached early adolescence. Use of these relational terms seems to parallel the growth of logical thinking as described by Piaget (1928). He found children used *because* in three generally different ways and with different frequencies at ages between 3 and 9. The younger children used the 'psychological' type referring to motivations and intentions much more often than they used the 'causal' and the 'reason' types which involve explanatory and logical accounts. A 'psychological' example is *Look, he's laughing!—Why?—Because he wants to catch the apple.* A 'causal' example used by a 6-year-old is *It is broken because it wasn't properly stuck*; and a 'reason' example used by the same child is *No, it's a boat, because it hasn't any wheels.* Incorrect use of the term when other connectives were needed was illustrated by *The man fell from his bike because he broke his arm* and *I've lost my pen because I'm not writing.*

Carol Chomsky (1969) found that certain forms of complex sentences tended to mislead children of between 5 and 10 years. In *The doll is easy to see* children seemed to understand that the doll could see easily, rather than that it could easily be seen. In *Donald promises Bozo to hop up and down* they took it that Bozo should hop, while in *John asked Bill what to do* it was thought that what Bill was to do was in question. When pronoun reference was explored in such examples as *After he got the candy Mickey left, Mickey yawned when he sat down* and *He was glad that Mickey won the race*, and where the children had some choice as to whether the *he* referred to Mickey or some other character, they did not always choose as adults tend to do. In adult usage *he* in a subordinate clause has unrestricted reference; one identifies the referent by the sense. But *he* in the main clause is taken to refer to someone other than the named person in the subordinate. In our first two examples *he* could be Mickey, but in the third could not. It is, in fact, doubtful whether all adults observe this use at all times, and there is certainly a psychological bias towards assuming identity of reference, even in the unrestricted cases, unless it is obviously incorrect to do so. Children from 5 to 10 seem to show this bias more strongly. In her study Chomsky has actually chosen forms that tend to go counter to even more general expectations, namely *The subject of a verb immediately precedes it* and *Name first, pronoun later*. Usages that go against these would take time to be learned, especially if they were rarely encountered, and it is not surprising that misunderstanding can arise. Passive constructions are another example of use that goes counter to the *Subject first* expectation, so it should come as no surprise to find that children do not tend to use the full passive, and that even at 7 years they can be confused by it. Their general tendency is to make sense of whatever they hear, so when semantic relations within the sentence constrain interpretation they understand correctly; but where a passive form is acceptable if semantically reversed they are in trouble. They interpret *The ball was lost by Tom* as *Tom lost the ball*, but they are easily confused by *Bill was chased by Tom*.

Having explored the implications of expanding skill in the use of complex sentences as far as the expression of ideas is concerned, we can turn to the growth of vocabulary from the primary school years. New words referring to classes of objects in the world around us are encountered throughout life but, from the school years on, some of these refer to objects that we have never actually seen. For novel objects that the schoolchild can see and use, the learning of new terms is not difficult; though without repetition of the use of the term in relation to the object remembering may not be so easy. Vocabulary is enriched within what is valued in the curriculum, and a variety of terms relating to such activities as field and laboratory studies in the sciences, playing musical instruments, reading and writing, physical education and experimental 'number' work can be acquired. But the objects to which the teacher or learner may wish to refer are not always at hand. Field trips and visits to museums all help, but they cannot supply all needs, and even with the assistance of pictures and diagrams new terms may not easily be learned. What greatly facilitates such learning is the clear and imaginative description of the nature of the reference, and this is best done with good command of explicit and adequate sentence construction. In a defence of verbal learning Ausubel (1961) considers that as the child approaches adolescence he is cognitively and verbally less dependent on contact with the referent for understanding new terms.

More abstract words are, however, more demanding than those with concrete reference. This can be seen in the early school years with quite simple words, and is reflected in the relative proportions of such words expected of children at different ages in standardised vocabulary tests. The author once overheard a conversation between a woman and her granddaughter on a bus. The child seemed to be about 5 years old, and was watching the unloading of some new post-office vans from a transporter. The conversation was about one van being unloaded, and part of it went as follows:

Child: What's that on the roof?
Grandmother: That's a ladder-rack. They put it up and climb the ladder to reach telegraph poles and telephone wires.
Child: It's going by the others.
Grandmother: Yes, they're building a fleet.
Child: (after longish pause) Grandma, what's a fleet?
Grandmother: It's when you have more than one or two. You can have a fleet of ships or buses or vans. A fleet's about twenty.

Here we have two attempts at definition of a new word. The first rests on the assumption that the grandmother was correct in taking it that the child was asking about the ladder, but the previous conversation had given her plenty of justification. Sharing the same seen referent, then, it was necessary only to give it a name. That some explanation of its use was also given was an added bonus. The second definition has no ostensive sharable referent; it requires not a naming but a description of use of the term. The grandmother makes a good job of it, making it clear that it relates to a variable number of objects and that these objects are of a particular kind. The child may or may not realise that they are all forms of transport, but she has enough clear definition to start or add to her understanding of the word. This definition required several sentences, however, though they were kept simple enough to be useful to such a young child.

It is probably true to say that no one instance of use fully defines a word, and it is clear that children's usage may not give as complete a coverage as that of adults. Throughout the middle school years children are learning to use abstract concepts such as *honesty* and *volume*, concepts which require definition through extended verbal description and complex mental operations. The work of Piaget and others who have taken up his explorations has shown that behind the acquisition of terms such as *area, speed, acceleration, distance* and *fraction* there lies a steady growth in mental power. The concept of *density* once provided the author with an interesting observation. Now this concept may be approached scientifically in two ways. In the first it is defined in terms of mass per unit volume, and the densities of substances are measured relative to each other and to that of water. Piaget's experiments and observations show that children do not master all the relevant concepts of *mass, volume* and *ratio* until they approach adolescence. When he asked children to compare the sinking and floating of different-sized pieces of iron and wood, those of 11 or so showed that they could consider the relation between weight and volume, but those of between 5 and 7 years tried to account for the sinking or floating in terms of only one dimension at a time, thus failing to explain why the small piece of iron sank while the large piece of wood floated. There is, however, another way of approaching the concept of density and that is to consider the particle structure of the substances. Now one child of 6 years, observing the sinking and floating as in the Piaget experiment, said *The wood always floats because it isn't so much squashed together, and the iron sinks because it's very squashed together*. It was possible to introduce this child to the word *density* as how much squashed together a substance was, which was, of course only a beginning to his understanding but nevertheless an aid to the expression of ideas he was already developing.

Through the later school years in adolescence children are introduced to a much wider vocabulary of the technical terminology of different 'subject areas' in the curriculum. But what of their mental organisation of words at this stage? Some work by Peel (1971) shows that the sort of semantic category systems we referred to earlier may still be developing, for he reported a trend towards fuller mastery of superordinate class concepts between 12 and 16 years, and in some cases continuing into adult life. He used test items like the following first giving full examples and then asking children to complete the others. Full examples were *Ford—car—vehicle* and *Westminster Abbey—church—building*. When given *Harrogate—town—?* and a choice of the five items *Yorkshire, city, population centre, local government* and *health resort* to fill the gap, it was only adults who predominantly made the correct choice of *population centre*. Twelve-year-olds tended to choose either *Yorkshire* or *city*, while 16-year-olds scarcely did any better. It is interesting to consider what sort of thinking they might have been using. One possibility is that only one of the leading items was attended to and the child shot straight from *Harrogate* to *health resort* (*Ford* to *vehicle*). Another is that both were attended to but not in the desired way. Maybe the thinking was *Harrogate is a town. A city is like a big town* (*a Ford is a car. A vehicle is a sort of big car*). The example may have been ignored or forgotten, the child saying simply, *Harrogate is a town in Yorkshire* or

There are local government offices in Harrogate. Local government is something to do with towns. These patterns are reminiscent of the word association skills of the 5-7-year-old, and maybe the tendencies to organise words in these ways persist through life, interfering with the semantic classifications into subordinate and superordinate categories. Learning such classifications cannot be particularly easy, however, and in order to explain to a child why *population centre* is the preferred answer in the above task a good deal of complex verbal expression is called for. Incidentally the adolescents did rather better with another test item *Bobby Charlton—footballer—?* in which at all ages *sportsman* was preferred to *Manchester United player, English International, bald-headed man* and *brother of Jackie Charlton.* Nevertheless the 12-year-olds did make rather more incorrect choices, tending to select *Manchester United player.* This fits neatly into thinking *Bobby Charlton is a footballer who plays for Manchester United.* Greater familiarity with the term in use may have led to more correct choices of *sportsman* than *population centre,* but we should not forget that we can never tie in thinking with verbal expression in a one-to-one manner. It may be that some of the correct choices were made on a basis of 'incorrect' thinking!

So far we have tended to speak of children's mastery of the literal use of speech, mostly in situations that bias it towards the mundane, but a proper understanding of the language includes the grasp of analogy and metaphor. Many of the insights of the past are tucked away into our everyday usage, so that we speak of the wind howling or someone's heart being in his mouth without realising the metaphor. People bark, run like the wind and sometimes reach their peak of fitness. The language of hymns and of the prayer book is full of illuminative metaphor, and the understanding of such forms requires not only the ability to make intuitive or explicit analogies but also the sharing of such use with others. Sometimes we produce metaphor that is at least infrequently encountered and may even be original in the sense of never having been produced before. A small study recently carried out in Leeds (Bambridge, 1975) suggests that children may be led into expressions of simile over and above forms in common usage quite early in their school lives, but that fairly original use of metaphor is not easily induced until rather later. It was found to be more common in adolescence than in the early primary school years and in those who read well than in those who did not. While teachers of very young primary school children also report examples of simile and metaphor in the poems and writing of their pupils, it is worth bearing in mind that there is a difference between the happy chance of illuminating associations made under conditions of encouraged free-ranging talk or writing and the ability to select an instance that is apt in relation to some intended expression. Here, of course, we have shades of what is meant by creativity. Is it enough to produce a wide range of unusual ideas or must one also go on to select and apply them in some enterprise? The former requires a well stocked and free-ranging mind, the latter a perception of relevance and an act of judgement.

A further and most important aspect of language development is the learning of different forms of expression and the contexts in which it is appropriate to use them. Recent studies in socio-linguistics have brought this matter to the fore, showing how in different social contexts different forms of language are expected. Many examples, however, are drawn from adult usage, and there is little to show how children learn the customs of their language community. We may, nevertheless, be clear about what it is they do learn. First, as Ferguson (1959) so clearly describes, it may be that two varieties of the same language are learned. One is used in such formal contexts as religious, educational, governmental and 'serious' communication situations; the other is used in informal conversations, instructions to social inferiors, folk literature and light entertainment. As a consequence of these differences young children encounter the informal variety as the language of the home, and not until they share in the wider social contexts do they find use of the formal variety. Nevertheless, it may be that more than one informal variety exists and that, as the Opies (1959) have reminded us, children of school age may use a playground variety that is different from both the formal and informal kinds they observe in adult use. Moreover, even where one formal variety is shared among a people, several informal versions may be in use within different subsections. These may be geographically or socially distributed, or both. Ferguson claimed that the formal language differed in both vocabulary and grammatical structure from the informal, there being more markers of distinctions of case, number and gender in nouns, and of tense and mood in verbs. He also remarked that it is unlikely that the later-learned formal version will come as readily to the tongue as the informal variety learned in early childhood. If that is the case then differences in exposure to the formal might lead to variations in competent usage, although speaking is more likely to be affected than comprehension. Since children in school are being introduced to more occasions of use of formal or standard versions of the language, it is to be expected that there will sometimes be failures to match the language variety to the context. This may be seen by teachers as evidence of poor language ability rather than of lack of social learning; while the children may find formal use odd, alien and even undesirable. There is some danger that mismatch will result in critical and even antagonistic interpersonal attitudes that are detrimental to learning.

Well before the current interest in socio-linguistics, Watts (1944) had devised a test of children's abilities to use appropriate forms of speech in different contexts. For example, he listed several social situations in which a speaker might ask another person to shut the door, and then he gave examples of how the request might be worded. These varied from the abrupt order to the courteous request, and from the affectionate asking to the formal requirement. Children were asked to match the expressions to the situations, and a clear developmental trend was shown, but the average number of correct matchings at the age of 10 was only three from a total of seven. The mastery of the appropriate use of language in social contexts depends as much on social learning as on linguistic skills, and we would be foolish to expect young children not to act inappropriately in novel situations. We should remember that interactions with teachers and other pupils in school figure largely in the category of new encounters for the 5-7-year-olds, and even for older pupils at transitions from one school to another or one teacher to another. Moreover, social gaffes and misunderstandings may be at least as embarrassing and inhibiting for them as they are for adults. How much worse must their feelings be if they are also made to feel unintelligent!

In this chapter much more has been said about the younger schoolchild than the adolescent, mainly because the teenager's abilities rapidly shade into those of the adult; but at all ages individual differences in competence, and variations in the pool of experience from which the children learn, lead to differences which must be taken into account in any full discussion of language and instruction. The model we built up in the first chapter took us from instruction of the individual to teaching in the classroom. We must now consider the differences between children likely to be encountered by the teacher.

3

Different Experiences of
Language Learning

Each child's learning history is unique, and his particular combination of personal qualities, social encounters and cultural experience not only helps to make him as a person but also fashions his use and understanding of language. Indeed it is impossible to separate speaker and speech, and since differences between persons may well affect educational processes it is important to consider how they arise. First, we shall examine the differences in ability that are related to language learning; secondly, we shall consider the distinction between deprivation and adequate experience; thirdly, we shall discuss differences both between and within social class; and fourthly, we shall treat social dialect differences.

If views that language acquisition has a strong cognitive base are at all valid then we might reasonably expect there to be widely different language abilities at any one age level. Moreover these differences may be quantitative, as in size of vocabulary or length and complexity of sentence, or qualitative, as in the different kinds of word and structure used. In teaching and learning we may well bear in mind that differences in the intellectual power children bring to bear on making sense of experience will be reflected in their understanding and production of speech. It is currently fashionable to speak more of cultural than of intellectual differences, at least in part because intelligence testing has been so badly understood and so grossly misused; but no teacher can escape the necessity of trying to understand and engage the intellectual powers of his pupils. He must treat their language abilities similarly, not only because these are intimately related to intellectual grasp but also because they are the ground of access to public knowledge.

It is probably more useful for our present purposes to forget about intelligence test scores and to consider instead the ways in which children respond to questions and problems. Although two children may obtain the same total score it is most unlikely that they will score identically throughout the test. They will have learned different items in the vocabulary sample. One may do well at seeing hidden patterns in a fixed visual array while the other may be better at constructing three-dimensional models. One may be carefully attentive but unable to hold a task in mind while the other may find it hard even to attend to the tester. Once we become aware of this we may well think it more profitable to observe children learning rather than to test acquired skills. Those psychologists who are particularly interested in the less able children have done valuable work of this kind, identifying differences in various sub-skills in discrimination and learning tasks (O'Connor and Hermelin, 1962). They have shown deficits in memory and attention to be important contributory factors in intellectual handicap. While in severely subnormal children the causes may be known to be brain lesions or congenital conditions, in the less handicapped the causes are obscure and there is no clear-cut dividing line between the normal and subnormal and no clear absence of relative disability in the normal. Moreover, poor attention may also be learned in some conditions of upbringing; Burt (1937) was inclined to associate this with poverty, whereas he thought that memory defects were less clearly socially or environmentally based. Wherever there is some relative disability children need either more practice or more distinctive cues to aid their learning, and this is as true of their language learning as of any other. In general the basic vocabulary acquired by most children up to 5 years of age is also learned by the less able of comparable mental age, though for the severely handicapped some deficit results from their relatively limited experience. Word usage and word associations are similar for the normal and subnormal of the same mental age, but with increasing maturity differences become apparent. The more handicapped are less able to explain the bases on which they classify objects or pictures, whether these be 'concrete' like furniture or animals or abstract like number; yet they show that they can carry out such classifications. Inability to associate a verbal label with an operation leaves it less securely learned, and although the word may be articulated, and recognised as having been heard before, it is virtually meaningless. Luria (1961) has described the condition of the severely handicapped as one in which speech as a second 'signalling system' is divorced from the primary perceptual-motor system. Being able to articulate forms of language even in appropriate contexts, is not the same as being able to use them effectively to guide and control the thoughts and actions of oneself and others.

Fortunately most children are not thus handicapped, but some measure of disability and relative slowness in learning is fairly widespread. The close association between verbal skills and mental age is seen throughout the child population in that, although there is room for considerable variation, there is a high correlation between verbal and non-verbal scores on standardised tests. Whatever the causes of these intellectual differences (and the interaction of biological, social and environmental factors is a matter for much discussion), anyone who faces the task of instructing a child must needs adjust to his verbal skills.

If his job is to teach a class of thirty or so children of the same chronological age the range of verbal abilities is likely to be considerable. A class of 5-year-olds may extend from a 'verbal age' of 4 years to one of 8 years; a class of 9-year-olds from 7 to 14 years, and one of 13-year-olds from 10 years to adult 'verbal age'. Reflection on the mismatch between verbal skill and social maturity and on the kinds of verbal skill described in the last chapter will serve to make plain the magnitude of the task of using language effectively in the classroom.

However children use their intelligence in developing language abilities, other factors will also affect their learning. It has already been suggested that the social and environmental conditions of a child's upbringing will have a powerful effect on his learning of both verbal and non-verbal skills. For some years now a considerable literature has been growing around the theme of social background and educational attainment, since it is evident that quite a strong correlation is found between social class and both test success and length of schooling. While social class, which is after all only a useful occupational classification scheme, cannot be regarded as a cause of relative success or failure, various features of upbringing which are to some extent associated with differences of occupation have been suggested as causal factors. Of these, early language learning has been heavily implicated. Useful discussion of work in this area can be found in a paper by Flude (1974), and in the work of Edwards (1976).

It has been argued on both sides of the Atlantic that early speech development in some social groups has been an inadequate preparation for schooling; but several educationally disadvantaged social groups are discernible in the literature, and they clearly do not present the same picture. Some are said to be deprived of language experience, while others have adequate but different learning. First we can identify groups so economically disadvantaged as to be severely constrained in their everyday lives. Of these we must distinguish between recently immigrant, relatively unabsorbed groups, and impoverished native speakers, since there are pronounced cultural and linguistic differences between them. Then we must take the stable but semi-skilled manual working class, corresponding roughly to the UK Registrar General's social class 4. Children from this group suffer less educational disadvantage than those from the first group, but they do not achieve as much in schooling as do the children of the skilled manual workers, who are likely to appreciate training as a means to increased income; and these in their turn do not tend to do as well as the children of fathers whose occupations require some skill with words, whether in clerical activity or managerial or professional posts. The different life-styles, values and aspirations of these groups are likely to be reflected in different emphases on the value of various language skills to their offspring. Since maternal occupations, although often in different kinds of work, tend to reflect the same kinds of skill difference as do paternal, the effect on styles of upbringing will often be reinforcing. Insofar as occupational groups sample different subcultures they are likely to use styles of communication which reflect the modes of living and thinking within these cultures, and with these their children will be reared. It is obvious, therefore, that educational disadvantage may be related to other differences than those of language learning. The term 'cultural deprivation' is sometimes used in referring to the experience of children of the poorer sections of the population, but the implications of a lack of culture are not acceptable to all, and, although Bereiter and Engelmann (1966) vigorously defended its use as a relative rather than an absolute term, it tends to cause confusion, and 'culturally disadvantaged' is preferred.

The most severely disadvantaged are undoubtedly the most impoverished, and these are both immigrant and non-immigrant. Some work in Educational Priority Areas in Britain summarised by Halsey (1972) makes clear one aspect of the language differences between such groups. His graphs of vocabulary scores show that immigrant children have very low scores, and only a small proportion attain values approaching the age norms for the tests. The native speakers of English obtain scores with the kind of normal distribution expected with the tests, although the mean scores of groups of such children lie well below the age norms. The difference is one of unfamiliarity with what is a second language, only newly encountered and alien to the family, versus restricted experience within the native tongue. It is important to recognise this difference, for different instruction is required by the two groups. It is a distinction not always made in the literature, especially in some of the American work on disadvantage where both kinds of children are grouped together for comparison with others and for consideration of compensatory language programmes. Deutsch (1967), nevertheless, is clear that important linguistic differences obtain, and sees these as resting not only in native language differences, but also in the totality of communication styles related to cultural differences. The distinction has been clearer in this country with its different history of immigration, and where some areas of cities are clearly populated by distinctive immigrant groups. Special training is being explored for teachers of English to immigrant children and their families. This training differs from that given to nursery school teachers and other workers with the economically deprived native-speaking children. As Halsey pointed out, very poor non-immigrant children seem likely to suffer vocabulary rather than linguistic deprivation, in that their experience of talking leaves them very much lost for words. They are not deprived of language as such, but of range within it. Creber (1972) illustrates their plight by giving teachers' reports of their language problems. Some of this loss may be more apparent than real, in that the child understands more than he is likely to reveal in his speech. He may be unable to comprehend the situation in which speech is required in school rather than to find the words to use. Labov (1969) has made this point very strongly in relation to judgements made by teachers and testers of culturally disadvantaged children in the United States. But whether special training should be directed towards helping such children to learn new forms, or to express themselves in novel contexts, or both, some effort to supplement relatively impoverished experience seems called for. Even so it must be recognised that no amount of supplementary provision can replace or compensate for the reduction of health and variety of experience that accompanies poverty, especially in the hearts' of our big cities.

Much of the argument that social class differences in use of language contribute to variations in educational attainment has not been based on studies of the really impoverished, however, but on comparisons between children of unskilled and semi-skilled manual workers and those of clerical, managerial and professional groups. Differences in vocabulary and grammatical structure in children's speech have been noted as associated with social class differences in several studies in the last fifty years on both sides of the Atlantic, but they were thought to lie in variations in intelligence, in schooling and in adult speech. In the last decade or so, however, the work of Bernstein and his colleagues has suggested that social differences can themselves be causal. Bernstein's work has now been heavily criticised, and it is useful to try to indicate what has happened.

First he made affirmations about linguistic differences between social classes, his emerging thesis being that social class subcultures determined thinking and behaving within them, which in turn determined the forms of language in use. Many have taken these early statements as truths without examining their base. The empirical studies which were developed to test the thesis had the effect, however, of forcing Bernstein to keep reconsidering the definition of his terms, as will be seen below. Moreover rather than taking a cross-section of social classes to investigate language use Bernstein concentrated on a comparison between lower working-class and middle-class groups of children. Criticisms have therefore ranged from attack on what is seen to be confusing change in terminology to more fundamental analyses of Bernstein's ideas and of the consequences of his choice of polarised groups.

In an early paper Bernstein (1960) pointed out the vocabulary differences between adolescent boys of similar non-verbal ability from these contrasted backgrounds, claiming that the verbal differences must be due to social not intellectual factors. But, considerations of test error apart, this is not very helpful. Firstly, it is odd that he regarded verbal intelligence as reflecting socio-cultural differences whereas he accepted non-verbal as being common ground. Secondly, any discrepancies were still only shown to be associated with social class rather than caused by the social milieu. It would have been useful to have shown that the two groups had experienced real differences in opportunities to learn and in the manner of learning the relevant items, and possibly even to show that they had different vocabularies, each showing signs of a unique internal structure. What was actually shown was that they spoke the same language, but that the working-class boys had a poorer command of it. When comparing the groups it might also have been worth considering that by adolescence much learning may have taken place outside the home language. Since vocabulary tests tend to tap more abstract and unfamiliar words beyond a mental age of 7 or so, one might wonder about the relative importance of the language of the home compared with that of the school, the mass media and private reading. If the latter influences are important it is still possible, of course, as Bernstein claims later, that aspects of upbringing incline children to respond differently to these sources of learning; but, while we may hold opinions on these matters we have little to go on in attempting to make informed judgements.

Bernstein later turned to questions of differences in the structure of speech as used by different social groups. He considered forms of speech in relation to their function and predictability for the speaker and listener; but this was not entirely clear in his early work, which tended to give the idea that lower working-class children used only a limited *public code* of speech related to social behaviour within the family or work group, while middle-class children had access to a more complex *formal code* used for a wider range of functions. Later the terminology was changed to *restricted* and *elaborated*, and in a fairly recent paper Bernstein (1971) has claimed that he might have avoided much misunderstanding if he had spoken of socio-linguistic rather than linguistic codes, for more was involved than language differences between social classes. What was at issue was whether there were subcultural differences in various kinds of thinking and of social behaviour which determined the forms of speech adopted. The restricted and elaborated codes were not to be identified with social classes, but the question of how each class drew on them was the nub of the matter. The restricted code implied selections of communication patterns characteristic of situations where much could remain implicit, where shared understanding led to relatively little being said—and that in a comparatively simple and possibly grammatically incomplete form. The elaborated code implied explicit speech wherein what was said had to be full and clear if understanding was to be achieved. This is the code of public communication when common experience cannot be or is not assumed. It is clear then that Bernstein's use of the term *code* is potentially very misleading. First, especially when connected with social class polarisation, it suggests two different languages rather than two emphases within the same. Second the actual term suggests a form of language rather than a regular system of selection of expression within a language. Bernstein's use of *socio-linguistic code* does not clear the possible ambiguity: it merely points to his preferred interpretation.

I take it that this latter can be illustrated by reference to the ways a mother and child might draw on different codes according to the assumptions they make and the understanding they are attempting to achieve. When I, as a middle-class mother, am faced with a decision about my young son's behaviour, an exchange like the following is likely. *Can I go to the Soldier's Field with Martin? O.K. Back by five.* This is short and simple, and hidden within it are assumptions that they will play football and that consent has been given to telephoning Martin to arrange matters. It is only because the situation is not novel, and previous conversations have established the shared knowledge of what goes on, that so little is said. If, on the other hand, the lad were to ask, *Can I go to Bill's?* my reply would lead to a longer and fuller exchange; for I do not know of a friend called Bill, or where he lives, or how contact will be made, or what the two boys will want to do; and, being the sort of mother I am, I shall want to know. Our conversation will shift towards more full, complex and explicit expression. But this does not only happen in matters of agreement about behaviour. It occurs in the child's seeking information. *What's garden in French?* is taken to require an answer like *Le jardin* or *Where's the dictionary?*, and nothing more will be said unless one of us sees a further problem. When he has asked about God or infinity, however, he has conveyed by his manner and by continued talking that he wants some response that will require me to talk more fully and explicitly. In my turn I have felt inclined to do just that. We can and do shift between drawing on restricted and elaborated codes; but this is to use Bernstein's terminology, whereas I would prefer to say that we shift between different levels of explicitness according to the content of our conversation and the purposes it serves. Bernstein (1971) suggests four major areas of mother-child interaction—regulation, instruction, imagination and innovation, and emotional expression. Use of the elaborated code in one does not imply its use in others, and different social classes draw on the elaborated and restricted codes to different extents in different contexts. This position is the outcome of his changing definition of *code*.

In spite of the illustration of this idea, the link between language choices and modes of thought or control is rather tenuous. From observation of speech it would be difficult to say with confidence much about what lies behind it, yet this is what Bernstein and his colleagues have attempted to do. Early work (Bernstein, 1962) showed that middle-class adolescent boys used less predictable expressions than lower working-class boys in small group discussion, and that they also paused more frequently in a way that was taken to indicate planning while talking. Additional features were greater clause length and verb complexity in middle-class speech, and certain stylistic differences such as more use of *I think* ... by middle-class boys, and socio-centric tags such as *Wouldn't it?* and *You know* by lower working-class boys. Bernstein's colleagues have offered more evidence of social class differences in the taking up of less predictable and more complex forms of speech. Lawton (1968) extended the work with adolescent boys and also analysed speech in individual interviews directed towards different speech tasks. He found middle-class boys more ready to change the form of their speech in shifting from concrete description to abstract argument, but the change, though difficult, was not impossible for lower working-class boys. Henderson (1970a) found changes in the proportions of different form classes in the speech of 5-year-olds in switching from description to narration, with more change by middle-class children. Hawkins (1969) reported differences in the structure of noun phrases in speech referring to a series of cartoon pictures. The lower working-class children used more pronouns for reference, and used them in referring directly to the pictures (exophoric reference) than did the middle-class children. The latter referred more frequently to items already defined by nouns or names within their speech (anaphoric reference). The use of more nouns allowed middle-class children to develop their speech more elaborately, using more epithets and qualifying clauses. It seemed to be the case, not that the lower working-class children could not respond like the middle class in terms of the forms of language used, but that they chose not to do so in that kind of task, for in a separate study (Francis, 1974a) I reported no such noun phrase differences in story reproduction tasks. The tasks were too demanding to allow anything like accurate imitation; the children constructed their own versions, sticking to the meaning but not to the syntax. In this study children of both social classes used similar forms with similar frequencies, though the use of more elaborated phrases and fewer exophoric references increased with age from 5 to 7 years. In a further small study Harding (1975) has replicated the cartoon and story reproduction sampling and added a further task in which the interviewer first made a point of establishing informal conversation before asking the child to describe how he would make him a cup of tea if he visited him at home. In this study both lower working-class and middle-class children used fuller reference in the story reproduction, the lower working-class group used more restricted reference in the cartoon description, while both groups used restricted reference in the informal task. It would seem that the children adopted various forms according to their perception of the situation and their habitual use of speech in such situations. One possible interpretation of Bernstein's notion of codes, taking them to be selection behaviours, has received considerable if tentative support in these studies; but it is clear that interpretations which suggest that the social classes do not share a common language, or that elaborate linguistic forms are available only to middle-class children, are not tenable. It is equally evident that if educational disadvantage accrues from linguistic differences between social classes the explanation must rest in different habits of use in different contexts, not from different forms of language.

It may, of course, be that different language habits lead to differences in the rate of learning more complex forms, even in those contexts in which they are normally used. Practice over a wider front may lead to advantage for the middle-class child in whatever context speech is found. All the above research reports include information that suggests that even where complex speech is used, age for age the middle-class children show some advantage. A careful analysis of the children's stories in my own study (Francis, 1974b) showed no differences in amount of speech (fluency) between classes, but it did show significant differences in the clause complexity of sentences. In both social groups there was a steady increase with age in the complexity index, but for the lower working-class children the level was the equivalent of a 6-month age difference below that for the middle class. Nothing different was learned by the two groups, for they produced the same kinds of clause patterning, but the lower working-class children came to use the more complex combinations rather later than their middle-class age-mates. An attempt to match children for intelligence reduced the difference considerably, so that it could be that the 6-month lag was related more to general intellectual difference associated with occupational classification than to social class variations in language use and language learning. The question still seems open for investigation and debate, but whatever answers may be found it remains true that the children of the lower working class are rather less well equipped for the demands of formal education than those of the middle class. Their language learning is not as advanced, and they are less likely to draw on complex and explicit forms of expression. Their vocabulary is less well suited to the needs of schooling; and they may use expressions in contexts and ways unfamiliar to the teachers, thus earning possible disapproval and inaccurate judgement of their abilities.

Concern about differences between social groups should not blind us, however, to the lack of research across the total spectrum nor to the enormous variation within the groups already studied. To illustrate the latter the first two of the following stories are taken from middle-class 7-year-olds, while the second pair are taken from the lower working-class children.

'One day Kanga met Jumbo looking very sad. She said, "What's the matter?" And Jumbo said, "I'm going to the dentist to have a tooth out." Nobody likes having teeth out. But Kanga said, if you have magic teeth it is very exciting. She said that she knew a friend who said he had magic teeth, and when he had teeth out he put them under his pillow, and in the morning he had a sixpence there instead. Jumbo's face brightened when he heard this. And he went off to the dentist. And as soon as his tooth was out he asked if he could have it. He took it home in his pocket. And he was waiting all day for bedtime. As soon as he'd finished his tea he went upstairs. And he put the tooth under his pillow. And in the night Kanga came up to see if he had remembered about his tooth. And he was fast asleep. So she crept down quietly and out of the house. The first thing Jumbo did as soon as he got up next morning was to look under his pillow. And there was no sign of his tooth. But there was a brand new sixpence there instead. As soon as he was dressed he went off to tell Kanga all about it.'

'He had a magic tooth. And he had to have a tooth out. And when he had the tooth out he asked for the tooth. And he ran straight home. And he had his tea. And straight after that he went upstairs and put the tooth under his pillow. Kanga shouted up, "Have you put your tooth there?" And in the morning he looked straight under his pillow. And he couldn't see his tooth but a shiny sixpence.'

'One day when Kanga was walking down the road he met Jumbo. Jumbo was very sad because one of his teeth is loose. Kanga said, "Some people have magic teeth." And then Jumbo smiled. And then he went to the dentist. And his tooth was took out. And he went home. He put the tooth in his pocket. And then he waited and waited. At night, after his tea, he went upstairs and put his tooth under his pillow and went fast asleep. And then Kanga came up to see if he had put his tooth under his pillow. Jumbo was fast asleep. And then Kanga had a look under the pillow. And he had putten his tooth under his pillow. And then she tip-toed down the stairs like a mouse. In the morning Jumbo woke up. And the first thing he did was look under his pillow. And his tooth wasn't there, but a shining sixpence under his pillow. And then he went to tell Kanga that it was magic.'

'Jumbo went to the dentist's. And he were feeling sad. So Kanga came up and said, "I know someone who said 'My tooth is magic'." So he had his tea. He went upstairs and went into bed. And then he put his sixpence under the pillow. Kanga come up. And then he were quiet as a mouse when he went down. And when he woke up there was a shiny sixpence under the pillow. Then he went to tell Kanga all the news.'

These examples are deliberately taken from the same model story so that the reader can make a fair comparison. The shorter two were not the skimpiest in either social group, but did seem to be those of children who were neither very dull nor very shy. The longer stories are from the more full, complex and explicit in each group, but are not the most complex in the total sample over two years and four stories. They are, however, representative of the more elaborated versions. The considerable differences between children within social groups are well illustrated, and lead us to consider the probability that they are not only related to personality and intellectual differences but also reflect different modes of upbringing which are as evident within social classes as between them.

Studies of the ways mothers bring up their children have been undertaken by other colleagues of Bernstein, and while they were designed to show social class differences they inform us of the ways in which speech skill differences can arise in different families. The research method involved was open to criticism, since it was based on mothers' reports of their own behaviour, and these might have been inaccurate and might have constituted a biased sample; but some small check on the validity of the findings was obtained by studying the children's subsequent behaviour. Studies by Henderson (1970b), Bernstein and Henderson (1969) and Bernstein and Brandis (1970) showed that mothers differed in the extent to which they claimed to engage in social chat, to talk about feelings, to explain rules of behaviour in terms of social relationships and to talk about ideas. They also varied in the extent to which they thought speech necessary for teaching children various skills, and in their reports of readiness to talk with their children in different situations. In general, middle-class mothers were more ready to cover a wide variety of use and were more concerned to encourage general cognitive skills than were the lower working-class mothers. Cook-Gumperz (1973) found that mothers reported different management techniques, in that middle-class mothers tended to use more verbal explanations of consequences of actions than did lower working-class mothers, while the reverse was true for brief controlling imperatives and non-verbal controls such as physical restraint and smacking. These findings compare with those of Newson and Newson (1970), and harmonise with those of Robinson and Rackstraw (1967), who found differences in reports of modes of answering children's questions. Middle-class mothers reported answering more fully, giving more factual information and more explanation. Two years later the authors found that the children of these mothers answered questions in ways similar to those their mothers had claimed to use with them (Robinson and Rackstraw, 1972). Turner (1973) also found that children, when describing cartoon pictures, used references to forms of behavioural control similar to those their mothers had claimed to use. Together, these studies throw light on some of the possible ways in which patterns of child rearing influence children's verbal behaviour. It is evident that much is likely to depend on several aspects of maternal control, some of which may be part of the way of life associated with certain occupational groups, but many of which will be found in mothers of all social classes.

The importance of the amount of mother-child communication in infancy and early childhood was first underlined in studies comparing children in institutions with those brought up at home. The considerable differences in speech and cognitive skill led to improvements in institutional care which gave each child more individual and sustained attention in care and in play. More recent studies of early mother-child behaviour have shown what Schaffer (1974) called the massive amount of care given to infants irrespective of social background, but they have also shown considerable variation in the kinds of communication patterns developed between mother and child. Schaffer noted how important was the mother's attention to the baby's behaviour and the intuitive timing of her speech and actions in relation to his:

'As part of an intensive investigation of mother-infant interaction that he is carrying out, Richards (1971) has reported on some film sequences he obtained of mothers and babies smiling at each other—just that. But when he then carried out frame-by-frame analysis he found two things: first, the infant's behaviour in this situation goes through a definite sequence: he would, for example, be quietly attentive while the mother smiled, he would then gradually become more and more active, pumping himself up as it were, and at the point of maximum "pumpedupness" he would pause a moment—and then he would smile. And the other thing Richards found was that what the mother did during this time had to be carefully phased to the infant's behaviour. For example, it was important that at the point of maximum "pumpedupness" the mother for her part should stop all activity, giving the infant time, so to speak, to smile. If she did not do so, if instead she continued to bombard the infant with stimuli in an unphased fashion, then the child would become tense and fretful and eventually begin to cry instead of smile.'

This quotation illustrates Schaffer's point well, and he continues to discuss examples of the mother's pacing her actions to tune into the child's. The author's own experience of recording her son's speech for a time at 2½ years was of a considerable gain in insight into his learning, and of an awareness that those in the family who successfully engaged him in dialogue were adjusting the timing as well as the structure of their remarks. It is likely that maternal patience, perceptiveness, and willingness to adjust to the realities of a child's behaviour are associated with variations in the scope and speed of learning to talk. Ervin-Tripp

(1971) summarised some of the studies of the patterning of maternal speech. It is clear that mothers do tend to accommodate their speech to communication with their toddlers, talking with them in shorter, more concrete, more complete utterances than those they use with older children or adults. Moreover, they speak more slowly and use different stress patterns. Observed mothers have mostly been middle-class, and they have tended to meet their children's needs in ways which suggest a very complex set of implicit assumptions and understandings of their actions, speech and thought. It would appear possible that mothers vary considerably in their ability to engage in such communication, and that some may well adopt more stereotyped and less flexible patterns of talking than others.

How far maternal speech actually determines the development of the child's is a moot point. It is evident that the child attempts some copying when he has learned to imitate to achieve his ends (Guillaume, 1926), that he may make an approximate rather than an accurate job of it, and that such a strategy may well apply more to learning new words than to acquiring new constructions; but the latter possibility cannot be ignored. Cazden (1972) looked at research findings that suggested some positive, though not very strong, relation between the structure of maternal speech and that of the child's, but the connection seemed to be made through mutual understanding and shared use rather than by what might be termed imitation. What the child learns from the mother is a complex of how to say what he wants to say when and where and to whom he wishes to say it. Behind differences in children's learning there lie, then, not only variations in the personal qualities of mothers, but also differences in the learned attitudes and values towards social relationships that are brought into the mother-child interaction. These in their turn must rest in involvement in the family unit.

Thus we come to consider other factors that tend to encourage or defeat optimal learning and so produce differences in children's abilities. Where a mother values the acquisition of some skill by her child she will tend to be more involved in talking with him in that area of skill. Cook-Gumperz, as already reported, found that mothers varied in the amount of talking in different fields of the child's experience and also valued these areas differently. Maternal interest is likely to give the child the vocabulary and speech structures associated with the valued behaviour, and the greater the interest the more language use the child will experience. Such interest has more opportunity to flower, however, if the conditions of family living are such that it can expand—if opportunities to use playthings, the media, books, and visits to a variety of people and places can be realised. In the home and outside it communication skills can grow apace with the mother's guidance and mediation. Most normally intelligent children given adequate experience become quite sophisticated little language users by the time they reach school. Their problems in adapting to schooling are not due so much to differences in level of ability to talk as to differences in the pools of experience in which they have learned—pools in which they continue to swim throughout childhood.

But within them lurk the hazards that can hinder learning. When a mother's attention to her child is reduced by such factors as poor health, a difficult household to run, a relatively low level of general competence, or the demands of other children or adults, then the frequency and scope of talking with the particular child may well be reduced. If her interest in the child's learning is also low then perhaps this is even more of a hazard. Deutsch (1967) investigated with others the factors associated with the cumulative deficit in vocabulary and ability measures shown by some children over the school years. They found that some factors characteristic of family life rather than social class acted over and above social class effects. These were dilapidated dwellings, low parental aspirations for children, large family size, lack of child involvement in family talking, and lack of variety in experience. One of our problems in considering disadvantage, however, is that we do not know what constitutes enough experience for any particular kind of language learning, so that a comparative disadvantage may not in fact result in a comparable deficit in learning. Moreover, although various studies tend to show correlations between such hazards as we have described and poor language development, these are not particularly high and many apparent disadvantages are surmounted through compensatory strategies within the family. It is perhaps well for the teacher who receives the child in school to remember not only the regularities reported in the literature, but also the counter-examples in the children he teaches. Let us mention a few.

Martin, of social class 5 but an only child, performed very creditably but without enthusiasm in the vocabulary test he was given, until we came to the item *Mars*. Most of his classmates had managed to define it as a Mars bar, but not Martin. With a sudden radiance he said, 'That's a good question', and proceeded to talk at length about his interest in astronomy. Sheila, of social class 4 and a moderately sized family, was an exceptionally good talker and reader. The family was strongly religious and she frequently attended Sunday School. Her home reading experience was of mother reading from the Bible. Peter, social class 1 and an only child, scarcely spoke at all and seemed very immature, but he was unfortunate in his emotionally disturbed parents. Jane, on the other hand, of social class 3 came from a family of six children but spoke and read well. Learning experiences vary enormously between families, and complex patterns of advantage and disadvantage cut across social class.

In speaking of speech differences we have not yet touched upon social dialect—ways of speaking that distinguish social as distinct from geographical groupings. Now this may be a particularly important aspect of speech since it is readily discernible and may easily provoke reactions between teacher and pupil that affect children's attitudes to language and learning. Dislike or disapproval may follow difficulty in hearing or signs of impatience or intolerance of difference. Two features are particularly interesting—how the dialect sounds and whether it seems to carry grammatical errors.

The sound of speech in itself conveys nothing; it is what it means to the hearer that counts. Even geographical dialect differences can provoke strong reactions. I can well remember my maternal grandmother's disapproval of my vowels which indicated that I did not come from her particular part of the country. She thought she was doing me a service in drawing my attention to my speech, but she simply made me rather self-conscious and a little apprehensive. While social dialect differences can also evoke negative emotional reactions, there is an additional danger of a certain kind of stereotyping, that is of generalising from voice sounds to inferences about the person based on general expectations of people speaking in that way. If a particular dialect is associated with a lower social class the teacher may be inclined to expect relatively poorly constructed speech and low cognitive ability if he has been led to form the notion that such attributes are characteristic of the class. The able child with such a dialect will have to prove himself, while the less able child with a middle-class sounding voice may be judged to be slightly more skilled than he is. It is probably true that teachers do not know with any great accuracy what occupations most of their pupils' parents follow, but they do form judgements based on what they see and hear of the child (Nash, 1973). Social dialect helps to define groups of children rather than individuals and is thus particularly likely to influence judgement. Robinson (1972) reports a study by Seligman *et al.* (1970), that showed teachers' judgements of children's compositions and drawings to be affected by information about their speech (taped) and appearance (photographed). The voice was particularly influential in judgements of intelligence, while both voice and appearance affected judgements of the children's work. Whether such effects are found and continue after first impressions in real-life classroom contexts is not known, but first impressions can be very persistent.

The second aspect of dialect that may give difficulty in interaction is variation in grammatical rules. To the speaker of standard English, or a dialect that has the same rules, the inversion of *were* and *was* which is characteristic of lower working-class speech in Leeds might be judged incorrect. Whether or not his remark is accepted by his teacher, *I were goin' out, Miss, when they was goin' in* is perfectly correct for a child speaking that dialect. It accords with the regular practice of his family and friends and is characteristic of his speech. It is not an error in the sense of being a mistake in an otherwise different pattern; the usage just happens to differ from standard English. The same child is most unlikely to use an auxiliary *had* in a pluperfect tense construction, since his dialect gets by with the perfect. Both tenses are accommodated to the same expression, and the distinction depends on associated conjunctions and the sense of what is said. A pilot investigation by a student on one occasion showed that, of a group of young schoolchildren speaking that dialect, not one produced the auxiliary *had*, even in a direct sentence imitation task. It was as if they had not heard it. Their middle-class age-mates, however, both used it and imitated it.

While we may hope that social dialect differences may become better understood by teachers, many will find it difficult to respond equally to various forms. Moreover, they will feel some responsibility for showing that use of standard English is to be preferred in certain social contexts. How they do this without implying that some dialect features are in some sense inferior to others, and, by extension, that the users are inferior persons, is an important problem. A further problem relates to possible differences in learning techniques of non-verbal communication. Having related children's learning of spoken language to the general context of family experience we have implied that there may well be associated differences in other modes of interaction involving the expression and interpretation of various kinds of message. This is a neglected area of research, but certain suggestions can be made; and what might be communicated in parallel with, and supplementing, verbal communication will be considered in a further chapter. Meanwhile we will examine further the relationship between language and learning.

4

Talking for Learning

In the last two chapters we have explored children's language learning so that we can estimate what expressive skills teachers might tap, and what children might understand from adult speech. Now we are ready to consider how their language skill, and that of their teachers, might be engaged in learning. If we continue with our view of learning as the construction of personal knowledge rather than the passive reception of 'facts', we can first examine the nature and role of verbal guidance in learning, and then see what scope it has in teaching styles. Discussion of actual classroom exchanges is deferred to the next chapter.

From our description of learning to talk it is clear that in any new learning both verbal and non-verbal aspects of communication may be involved. They may come together, or some marginal advantage may lie with one or the other in any particular situation. They may aid the grasp of a problem or the advent of a new insight, but new learning may also require the extension of language skill. Even before words are recognisably used by the child verbal and non-verbal cues from the mother seem to aid learning. Newson (1974) argues that infant understanding is not based solely on the baby's direct experience of the world around him, but also on the way this experience is patterned and directed through the caretaking activities of the mother:

'The social programming to which normal infants are ordinarily subjected, because it occurs as a natural consequence of the care which is necessary for the infant's biological survival, is both massive and continuous. Its effect is to break up the ongoing stream of disordered experience into temporal chunks with defined beginning and end points, and into event sequences to which meaning can be attached. Because these recur day in and day out, they become familiar to the child, who soon shows his recognition of them by motor anticipation—which incidentally provides feedback to the caretaker that at some level a message has been conveyed and reacted to. The two-way interaction process is characteristic. In fact the baby participates willy-nilly, whether at the level of being attracted towards events that someone has deliberately tuned to the vagaries of his own attention, or whether he is simply precipitated into massive physical, whole-body movement, as when he is picked up and changed by a caretaker. Response to mere inanimate objects in his environment must wait upon the development of his ability to explore and exploit them, by incorporating them into his own voluntarily initiated action sequences; and it may only be when these action sequences are in turn incorporated into interactions with persons, who can present these objects in ways which highlight meanings related to what can be done with them, that the child can arrive at understandable and communicable concepts such as size, weight, shape, colour, texture, solidity, deformability and all the myriad notions which we all learn to operate in our everyday anticipatory judgments about the world.' (Newson, 1974, p. 25)

This statement is based on research findings. Newson and Packer (1973) gave an extract from a video-taped recording of a mother and her 7-month-old baby playing with rattles. The major features of the episode were the infant's banging of a rattle on the table and the mother's taking up of this action with another rattle to create a shared playing of rattle banging. The establishment and maintenance of the game depended on motor action; but it was accompanied by vocal and verbal acts which helped to direct attention to moves and desired moves, and to encourage movement and the expression of feelings. An extract is given below:

'*Mother: You go bang with yours.* Tilly follows mother's rattle as she withdraws it from the table and holds it in her lap within Tilly's view. Mother brings back her rattle and repeats three bangs on the table with her rattle. Tilly watches mother's banging movements. Tilly continues to follow mother's movements as mother withdraws rattle to her lap again. Tilly looks at own rattle. While turning her rattle over in her hands, Tilly accidentally (?) knocks it against the side of the table. *Mother: That's not bang. It's only a little bang.* Tilly looks away in the direction of mother's rattle, knocking a plastic container as she does so. Mother knocks four times on the table with her own rattle. This brings Tilly's attention and gaze back to mother's rattle. Tilly looks at mother's rattle while sucking her own. *Mother: You're going to eat it instead, are you?* Tilly takes the rattle out of her mouth, and deliberately (?) bangs with her own rattle against the table six times with no rhythm. Mother says *Bang* to Tilly's bangs on the table. Mother bangs her own rattle on the table with accompanying *Bang, bang, bang.* Tilly watches mother's action of banging. Tilly repeats her banging sequence with her own rattle while mother says *Bang* to every act.'

And so the game continues with Tilly learning to take turns with her mother and making her own banging more rhythmic. It is clear that while the word *bang* is being tied to a particular action pattern, which gives some basis for meaning, other utterances are forming an interesting and encouraging background. One might argue that they could mean nothing to the child and were no more than extraneous noise, but that would be to miss the point that the mother was working to keep up the initial 'agreement' to play. As we pointed out in the first chapter, agreement on what is learned must be preceded and accompanied by agreement to engage in the learning exchange. Aspects of language play a part in both forms.

Gregory (1973) studied the ways mothers helped slightly older children to learn to put shapes into a form-board:

'Very early on, the mother is involved in getting the child to play with the board. She makes the board "rich", i.e. she makes it the focus of a large number of associated activities. She deliberately sets up events for the child in order to hold, maintain and guide his attention. Informal games evolve.... The mother does not set up activities separate from the child, but seizes on and utilises what the child is doing, and can do.... Later on in the learning sequence there is the act of getting the piece into a hole. Implicit in this activity is its termination, but the mother makes the act especially significant. There is a release in the tension of the situation as the piece goes in, often marked by saying 'Good' or clapping. For the child there must seem to be a gradual build up in tension which is released as the piece goes in.'

Here we see how verbal, accompanying non-verbal, signals can be used to guide the learning as distinct from conveying what is to be learned. They can signpost beginnings and ends and fruitfully guide the tension of learning. Other observations made in the Nottingham research unit by colleagues of Newson show the strategies mothers adopt with children from 3 to 5 when helping them to solve jigsaw puzzles. Guiding speech is very evident, though each mother-child pair has its own particular communication style.

Another insight into mothers' instruction of children can be gleaned from a study by Hess and Shipman (1965) of mothers from different social backgrounds teaching their 4-year-old children three simple tasks—toy sorting, block sorting on a basis of two characteristics, and design copying. The teaching styles varied considerably, as the following examples of remarks introducing the toy sorting task show clearly:

First mother: All right, Susan, this board is the place where we put the little toys; first of all you're supposed to learn how to place them according to colour. Can you do that? The things that are all the same colour you put in one section; in the second section you put another

group of colours, and in the third section you put the last group of colours. Can you do that? Or would you like to see me do it first?
Child: I want to do it.

Second mother: Now, I'll take them all off the board; now you put them all back on the board. What are these?
Child: A truck.
Mother: All right, just put them right here; put the other one right here; all right put the other one there.

Third mother: I've got some chairs and cars, do you want to play the game?
Child does not respond.
Mother: O.K. What's this?
Child: A wagon?
Mother: Hm?
Child: A wagon?
Mother: This is not a wagon. What's this?

The first mother made the task clear and gave specific verbal guidance about the basis of sorting. Although the expression *group of colours* seems ambiguous it posed no problem in that particular partnership. The mother looked for evidence of understanding, in this case non-verbal, and checked the child's feelings about doing the task before withholding further guidance and letting her try. The second mother began to demonstrate the basis of grouping, but without correcting the false cue she elicited verbally from the child, nor giving correct verbal guidance. The third mother gave no lead at all into the sorting, and reduced the verbal exchange to attempts to get the child to name the toys. Hess and Shipman found a marked tendency for middle-class mothers to behave like the first and for other mothers to be less helpful the lower their social class status. Not surprisingly, the middle-class children were better able to perform the tasks and to explain the basis of their sorting. One might ask how far the experimenters had been successful in instructing the mothers about their task, but this would take us into another problem—what different kinds of learning task mean to different parents and different social groups.

These studies of early learning show that before entering school it is possible for the child to have become familiar with many of the ways language can be used to facilitate learning—informing, expressing feelings, assisting, directing, confirming, testing, correcting and approving. In earlier discussion we have indicated something of the informing and expressing functions in maternal instruction, for while we were discussing language learning itself it was obvious that such learning went hand in hand with the growth of perceptual-motor, cognitive and social skills. Judgement as to what forms of speech are helpful and what are so much beyond the child as to be totally incomprehensible, misleading or discouraging is an art to be developed by the teacher. At its best it requires a good understanding, not only of the probable general features of a child's language skill, but also of the particular characteristics that derive from his personal experience.

In addition to observation of teaching attempts by mothers we can look to other sources for analyses of the ways language might be used to guide other forms of learning. Holding (1965) summarised and discussed some useful points arising out of research into training. Since this might include such skills as trouble-shooting, the analysis is not inappropriate for much of what is more usually termed education. If we consider that the nature of the learning to be achieved lies on a continuum of skills from the more specifically perceptual-motor, e.g. tracing and handwriting to the more cognitive, e.g. rule discovery and problem solving, we can see that any such learning requires a grasp of constituent parts and integration, planning, checking and smoothing of these in the total performance. How far symbolic representation is necessary or helpful in learning these skills is a matter that can be empirically explored. Holding took up three main issues in guidance—instructions, aid during learning, and knowledge of how well each performance is carried out. In all three it is possible to inform the learner non-verbally, as with physical demonstration and guidance or by signals or diagrams or charts, but verbal information has been shown to carry certain advantages. Verbal instructions are more easily memorised than others, particularly for complex tasks, because they take advantage of the prior experience of the learner that gives them meaning. If they do not recall relevant 'know-how' then either some additional training is needed or a different form of instruction is called for. For similar reasons verbal guidance or hints during the task are often more readily taken up than non-verbal; and in tasks where transfer of training from some other skill is helpful, the verbal definition of what is involved may help to focus attention on relevant features. Verbal guidance is not sufficient to develop skill, however, for although it may shorten the learning time needed, practice in the performance is essential. A further run-through always benefits from knowledge of the result of the last, and verbal description of the outcome has the dual advantage of conveying a variety of information with more lasting effect. Moreover, if feedback is delayed a verbal report is more likely to be related meaningfully to what was done than is a tick or a cross! In spite of these advantages it can nevertheless be shown that there are possible drawbacks to verbal instruction; but these tend to rest in inappropriate use. Individual learners are not equally able to take it up—older persons, for example, sometimes finding it harder than the young in industrial skills. This may be because 'translation' into activity is required, a process whose speed will vary not only with personal attributes, but also with the complexity of the task. In addition, the instructions might fail to be as clear and as simple as possible and thus lead to confusion or slow understanding; or the learner might simply not have the prior experience to use the information in them.

While the powerful coding properties of language make verbal guidance so useful in the teacher's hands, they can also be used to advantage by the learner for self-direction. Knowing what is to be attempted can lead to verbal encoding whether it be in thought, subdued muttering or even overt talking to oneself. Luria (1959) explored the young child's capacity to direct his own activity verbally as part of a developmental account of more general response to instruction. Apparently the very young child, under 2 years, is unlikely to be able to respond to a verbal instruction that conflicts with his tendency to repeat a previous action or that requires a choice to be made between the object of the instruction and some other object that interferes with access to it. For example, if asked to give the speaker a toy brick that lies before him the child may well hand over another toy if it happens to lie nearer. His ability to follow an instruction when no such conflict exists seems therefore to be less stable than we are inclined to believe. After 2 years the response to verbal instruction to attend in some way to specific objects seems to be firm, but there is considerable difficulty in responding to more complex instructions such as *When the bell rings, press the switch.* This is not very surprising in view of what we know of the child's language abilities; nor, in view of the repetition tendency referred to above, is it surprising that at the level of more simple instruction, when the child is told what to do *at the time of the signal,* he at first finds the inhibiting instruction more difficult to observe. The speech signal functions as a command to act 'positively' whether it is positive or negative. But it is surprising that the child's own spoken command to himself, conditioned appropriately to the signals, functions reliably only as the fifth year is approached. It seems, on the basis of this kind of work, that it is debatable how far language promotes learning or guides action in the early years and how far the learning or action guides the acquisition of verbal skills. This is a considerable problem when we turn to the more cognitive rather than the more perceptual-motor skills.

Suggested answers to the question of the place of language in such learning have been both varied and disputed. If we suggest that verbal expression aids the coding of recognised categories of experience, thus aiding memory, recall and problem solving, it might be argued that stored and available memories can be readily used without resort to verbal symbols. Kuenne (1946) attempted to throw light on this matter in an interesting set of experiments with children of about 2 to 3 years. For example they learned to find a sweet placed consistently beneath the larger of two squares of different sizes. They were then expected to find a sweet under one of another pair of squares, one of which was the same size as that under which the sweet had first been reliably found, while the other was larger. The question was whether the children would transfer their expectations to the same-sized square as before or to the one which stood in the same size relation to the other square of the pair. Since the size relationship was the criterion the sweet was to be found under the larger square. Those children who were observed to mutter such phrases as *under big one* or *big one* in their first learning found the second task much easier than did the others; but, when in a further experiment children were given prior training on a size relation task before trying to find the sweets under the squares, they performed just as well as the children who had shown that they could verbally encode the relation. Speech did therefore seem to aid thinking under the first conditions, but the second experiment suggested that while it could be useful it was not essential. We cannot know, though, how the children who did not speak were encoding their thinking and learning.

With more complex concepts Vygotsky (1962) was able to show how verbal labels acquired meaning. He used nonsense syllables to stand for the concepts which formed the rather difficult basis of sorting a set of coloured bricks of various shapes and sizes. Combinations of height and area of cross-section were the relevant attributes, and the bricks were labelled beneath with the chosen syllables. Children were shown the label on each brick after they had allocated it to a group, and if the grouping was incorrect the brick was reallocated until it was placed correctly. It was shown that whereas 5- or 6-year-olds could group the bricks according to single perceptual attributes such as *red* or *round*, the more complex basis of grouping was not grasped until the age of 9 or 10 years. Stones (1970) was able to show that the verbal label aided further sorting of different sets of objects possessing the same criterial attributes. Children who had sorted the Vygotsky bricks without the verbal labels were much less able to extend their skill to the different materials. These studies show that different kinds of thinking underlie children's use of different words, and that whatever has been encoded in the use of a particular word or set of words is potentially available as part of the ground for further learning.

The role of verbal self-guidance in adolescence was explored by Gagné and Smith (1962) in a review of studies of the use of language in problem solving. In their own work with adolescents they used a difficult problem—a game requiring a particular pattern of moves and with a specifiable minimum number of moves to the end. The pupils were allowed to practise simple, but similar, games; and they were fully informed about the materials of the game, its aim, and the minimum number of moves needed to achieve it. They were then divided into four equivalent groups, and each group was given a different additional instruction. One was to make a verbal statement of the reason for each move as it was made and to try to find a rule to tell some other person how to solve the problem. Another group was to make similar statements but not to find a rule. The third group was asked to find a rule, but was not required to explain the moves; while the fourth was not asked to do either. In general, both in terms of solving the problem and of formulating the rule, the groups that were required to explain their moves did better than the others; but the instruction to find a rule did not seem to have any appreciable effect by itself. Certain questions remained unanswered, however, for differences in the patterns of moves made by the pupils were not explored and the ways verbalisation helped were not clarified. Is it somehow easier to make a rule from repeated verbal statements than from repeated action patterns? And if so, at what ages would this apply?

So far we have thought about the use of language in guiding learning, but, because most human learning is the building and consolidation of skill or knowledge, we have necessarily touched upon the problem of the relationship between language and thinking. A long-standing controversy can be discerned between those who maintain that thinking largely depends on language and those who regard it as primary. To some extent the opposition of ideas diminishes when the ways in which proponents use their terms are examined, and this seems particularly true of the arguments of Vygotsky and Piaget, as can be seen in the latter's reply (1962) to Vygotsky's (1962) criticism of his earlier writing. Both had observed young children talking aloud while playing alone, but they attributed different importance to such monologue. Piaget saw it as fading away and having no great significance in the development of logical thought, while Vygotsky described the development of verbal reasoning as dependent on the meeting in monologue of early thinking and of early speech learned in social exchange—such monologue developing into inner speech and so into verbal thought. It is surely incontrovertible that speech develops in forms of dialogue, but its grasp depends on the ability to symbolise; and while Vygotsky stressed the social aspect Piaget explored the latter, claiming that language development was based on and related to the symbolic representation of experience in both enacted and imagined forms. For Piaget, the greater importance of dialogue was not in providing a language model but in informing the child of the viewpoints of others when he had outgrown his infant egocentrism, of which monologue was but one feature. The adaptation to other points of view was an important step in the growth of logical thought. It is clear from Piaget's reply to Vygotsky that a distinction must be made between verbal thinking and logical thought, and that the difference between the writers was more a matter of emphasis than of opposition. The difference should not, however, be lightly dismissed, for a reliance on one account rather than the other has implications for education. The Russian viewpoint of language as a second signalling system suggests that verbal skill may be additional to cognitive rather than derived from it, and that it may therefore be used to advance the latter, while the Genevan viewpoint suggests that language is so intimately related to other symbolising activities that it can only marginally advance thinking. In considering the implications for teaching and learning we should bear in mind that the Genevan work clearly specifies the development of logical thought against particular models of mathematical groups and propositional logic. It is debatable whether this can be said to encompass all that is involved in processes of thinking, and it may be that such thought is involved in different ways and to different extents in various learning tasks. Thus, while experiments which tend to confirm the Genevan approach are to be taken seriously as suggesting limitation in the use of language to promote the development of logical thinking, they should not be read as indicating that it has little facilitating effect in all thinking tasks.

The most important point at which the limitations of language have been shown is that of the transition from pre-operational to operational thought (to use Piaget's terminology) when the child is between 5 and 7 years of age. By 7 years children begin to assert that, in spite of appearances, certain operations do not alter some fundamental properties of matter and are reversible. Thus, pouring an amount of water from one container to another of different proportions, while altering the appearance, does not alter the amount, as will be evident if the water is poured back. Rolling a piece of plasticine into different shapes does not change the amount and the original shape can be reformed. Before they can confidently make such assertions children are said to be at the stage of pre-operational thought, and are also described as non-conservers in contrast with the conservers who see the unchanging properties. The non-conservers compare the appearance of water poured from one jar into another of different proportions with that of the same amount in a container identical with the first, and tend to say that there is more or less rather than the same amount. But conservers judge them to be the same, commenting on the identity of the poured water, the possibility of pouring it back, or the compensatory features (e.g. taller but narrower) of the shape of the second container. Bruner (1966) has pointed to the complexity of the judgements, showing that a grasp of the unchanging identity of the water is one aspect, but that the recognition of equivalence of amount through ideas of reversibility and compensation is needed to counter the tendency for perceptual evidence to outweigh the knowledge of identity. Non-conservers may mention any aspect of these judgements, but they do not grasp the whole. One might consider the step from pre-operational to operational thought as a movement towards a higher level ability to combine judgements. Bruner comments:

'... language obviously does not help him "put things together", nor is it adequate as a medium for communicating to an adult what the child experiences' (Bruner, 1966, p. 205). The term *the same amount* covers a complex of meanings which is not evident in any particular example of its use. For the child to use it therefore does not necessarily imply an understanding comparable to the adult's.

Sinclair-de-Zwart (1967) offered evidence that language training did not really help children not yet at the stage of operational thinking to express the relations involved in comparing objects on the basis of two criteria at once. Pencils in one group could be described as both longer and thinner than those in another group of shorter, fatter crayons. Children who gave independent evidence of attaining operational thought in conservation tasks tended to be able to express the relations between attributes of the pencils, but only those who were marginally conservers were able to improve their expression of comparisons after appropriate language training. For most non-conservers the training itself proved to be difficult, and the results showed no improvement. Furthermore, the language training did not help children to become conservers in a plasticine-rolling demonstration in which the relevant perceptual changes were the sort they had been trained to express. In a more recent account written with colleagues, Inhelder (1974) reported various attempts to facilitate the development of operational thought, including verbal training, but the latter was found to give only marginal help. Nevertheless it was concluded that language aided the expression of already acquired ideas; it tended to draw attention to specific features of tasks very usefully; and it could with some children give rise to limited correct solutions and with others just tip them over into operational thinking.

According to Piaget, another major change in thinking takes place in adolescence with the ability to make judgements in accordance with the requirements of propositional logic. Except for studies of the abilities of deaf children (Furth, 1966) which tend to show how adolescents without language skills can use some such thinking, there seems to be little work relating language to thought at this stage, though a study by Wason (1969) is of interest. He explored the difficulties encountered by young adults in solving a particular logical reasoning problem and reported that the task was not made easier by verbal cues and that insight did not readily occur even with full verbal explanation and discussion of the correct solution. The problem was to say which of four cards necessarily had to be turned over to find out whether the sentence *Every card which has a red triangle on one side has a blue circle on the other side* was true. Subjects already knew that a triangle on one side was always paired with a circle on the other, and that each symbol could be either red or blue. The four cards showed a red triangle, a blue triangle, a red circle and a blue circle; and the principal difficulty lay in realising that a red triangle might lie on the other side of the red circle—a circumstance which would falsify the sentence. A further difficulty was in realising that what lay behind the blue circle was irrelevant to the truth of the sentence. In view of later work (Johnson-Laird *et al.*, 1972) it seems possible that Wason did not hit upon the verbal guidance most likely to help the solution (though at the time that was not his aim), for perhaps some help was needed to deal with the arbitrary nature of the symbols. Johnson-Laird's subjects found the task much easier with pictures of envelopes and a sentence relating the stamp on one side to the sealing or lack of sealing on the other. Possibly Wason's subjects would have found an instruction such as *Consider carefully all the possibilities on the other sides* to be helpful, for some might have been tipped into formal thinking. An interesting question to which there are no clear answers is how it is that children and adults who show in some tasks that they are capable of a certain kind of thinking nevertheless fail to use it in others and also fail to make use of verbal cues and explanations to help themselves.

Having acknowledged the reservations of the Genevan school about the role of language in learning and thinking, we can nevertheless point to its enormous advantages in many major respects. Not only is it useful for guiding learning, but it is often the means of making learning manageable. Appropriate language encodes learning so that it can be stored, recalled and transformed to suit the further needs of the learner. In an article on learning and thinking Bruner (1959) pointed to the importance of encoding experience—learning in a generic way—in order to save ourselves similar learning in future. Such learning, he said, is like 'leaping over a barrier into thinking'. We can illustrate the point by considering a relatively simple concept like *bird*. For the 2-year-old this term may serve to refer only to a particular bird, or a memory of one, or any one of a small set of seen birds. For the 6-year-old it can be a term that encompasses several kinds of bird such that each kind has its own characteristics but all share some features in common. Once the term is grasped in this way it becomes a remarkably economical way of defining a new kind, never yet seen by the child. To say that a toucan is a bird is to say that it flies; it has a nesting place; it lays eggs; it has two eyes, two legs, two wings and a tail; it pairs to rear its young and so on. It is also to say that it is a special kind of bird that has its own defining characteristics which the learner will want to know about. Even here the knowledge embedded in the term is likely to give the child leads into the kind of question to ask about these features—question of colour, size, song and habitat. A term like *desert* will carry no meaning for an English pre-school child, but through pictures, stories and reading it will begin to acquire definition for the child of school age, and most probably will be thought of in relation to landscape features and particular examples of desert regions. In adolescence, however, it can be seen as a term for all regions with certain common climatic characteristics. Further, these latter may be systematically related to features of the earth's surface and orientation towards the sun; so that when a further term such as *grassland* is introduced as a similar kind of term the pupil does not have to learn again about these systematic relations but needs only to identify the climatic criteria of grassland regions to be able to predict their likely distribution. Words and their relationships in language give us command of a knowledge of the world that we could never build up without them, and Bruner's concern with the place of language in learning does have the merit of encouraging the instructor to have a more open mind about the use of verbal instruction than might be the case if he were heavily influenced by thinking about its limitations. The kind of language used must nevertheless respect the developmental limitations outlined in our second chapter.

From questions of the way language may aid the individual's learning we may turn to issues of the place of language in methods of instruction as advocated for classroom teachers. One of the consequences of emphasising the importance of the learner's active discovery of ideas and principles is sometimes to diminish the role of language as an aid to instruction—indeed even to underestimate the value of any kind of guidance. It is as if it is said that new ideas cannot be conveyed to children, that they must find them for themselves. But while discovery learning has much to commend it, it is not a simple matter. Educators have advocated various aspects, often, as in the cases of Locke and Dewey, seeming to base their views in part on analogy with scientific discovery, as if the latter rested on the individual's inference from observation or experiment without any scientific frame of reference or exchange of ideas within the scientific community. Thus discovery learning has sometimes been emphasised without due regard to the necessity of harnessing it to other learning or to agreed ends. It may even be an end in itself, and much infant and nursery school activity is seen as a kind of play experience in which discovery may take root. Play is seen as the natural learning context for the young child, but there is no guarantee that he will bring to school play the same urge to mastery and discovery that pervades his learning outside. Moreover, everyday learning outside school is more than a matter of pottering in the park or garden, running about the street, or playing with toys. Much is guided by other persons, whether adult or child.

It is interesting that the Montessori method of teaching, which numbers amongst its aims that of fostering the child's ability to discover regularity or pattern, does not leave discovery to chance. Bryant (1974) reported how he was surprised to find a Montessori teacher able to guide a 3-year-old to the construction of a diagonal on a kind of form-board, whereas the same task was not achieved unaided by many 5-year-olds. The particular technique used was that of not only showing the child the correct hole at each move, but also showing, by first placing the peg incorrectly and then shaking the head, the incorrect possibilities. This seemed to guide the child to the rules for placement in the diagonal without any verbalisation, but with well planned guidance. It is clear, though, that if the advantages of direction of this kind are admitted, then, as Dearden (1967) points out, discovery learning may be appropriately aided by verbal as well as non-verbal forms.

Unfortunately, advocates of discovery methods do not always make this clear enough; and they may even appear to set discovery in opposition to verbal instruction, the latter being reduced to merely telling the pupil definitions and rules. In recommending discovery methods Bruner (1961) claimed that they yield more personal and valued knowledge, greater intellectual power which lies in the ability to use strategies carrying more information, intrinsic motivation towards competence and mastery, and personal strategies facilitating memory and recall by linking personal forms of past learning with the present. While the rest of Bruner's work allows us to assume that he would spell out and appreciate the ways in which verbal guidance might be involved in discovery methods, he nevertheless contrasted the latter with the 'expository method' which is taken to be verbal instruction with the student as a passive recipient. Consequently it is easy for the undiscerning to slip into the error of contrasting discovery with verbal instruction rather than with passive reception.

Attempting to disentangle some of this type of confusion, Ausubel (1961) wrote an essay in defence of verbal learning. He separately contrasted reception with discovery and rote with meaningful learning, warning against the confusion of rote learning with receptive learning, for the latter can be active as well as passive. An exposition or a rule can be anticipated, mentally chewed over, critically examined and satisfyingly incorporated into personal knowledge; it need not be swallowed as an indigestible whole. Verbal practice has a place in learning, a consolidating function, whether it be to firm up something that has already been grasped in its essentials or to define more firmly the array from which further insight can be obtained. Rote learning without understanding is not a consequence of verbal instruction but of bad teaching, and it is the latter which has discredited the former. Ausubel was thus very concerned to say that verbal learning should go far beyond such minimal techniques as rote memorising and parrot-like recitation, and, while appreciating the necessity of concrete experience as a fundamental basis for learning, he indicated that to depend solely on this and its concomitant problem-solving discovery methods would be to restrict the child within the bounds of his own concrete experience. With a sound basis of concrete learning, however, one could venture to use verbal material in meaningful forms of receptive learning. 'Meaningful' implied that the materials, the process and the outcome should make sense to the learner; that, starting on familiar ground with an orientation towards extending comprehension, the learner should be able to master and retain new knowledge set securely in his previous experience but stretching well beyond it. The adolescent could be expected to profit extensively from such instruction, but at no age is appropriately worded teaching ruled out. This recipe for meaningful receptive learning sounds not unlike what might be recommended in guided discovery. This is necessarily so if one accepts that good teaching involves verbal guidance in some form, and that learning involves discovery within as well as without verbal expressions. The more interesting question for education is not verbal brainwashing versus discovery, but how language may be best drawn on to help the learner in the classroom.

In the actual process of learning children can be encouraged to restructure problems, to produce relevant suggestions and to check their own solutions. This is as true for the task of grasping the meaning of a poem as for relating events in history or solving an algebraic problem. But it is more easily said than done. Even with an inspired choice of materials to suggest restructuring, it is often the case that the learner 'jams' on one line and on one hypothesis. Some flexibility is needed, and this is most easily encouraged by social and verbal intervention. The observation that other children have different ideas is helpful, but often some verbal expression of alternatives seems to be needed to help the child make the mental transformation to a new structuring. Verbal expression of the desired end of the learning, including reminders when needed, also helps to encourage relevant ideas whether they be convergent or divergent. Extending learning to real-life problems outside the classroom may also benefit considerably from verbal exchange. Children's verbal reports of external visits or experiences give the teacher some insight into the manner and extent of their understanding, while imaginative construction and analogy assist the comprehension of the external world from the classroom context. No matter what gestures, actions, pictures, diagrams and models might be used, verbal communication is essential for normal speakers to tap each other's knowledge and imagination, and that of writers and artists of various kinds, for any significant learning that might be termed education.

If guiding learning is to entail the promotion of a confident approach, as the advocates of discovery methods suggest, then much will rest on the wise selection and ordering of materials and concepts to do justice to the logic of what is to be learned and to the pupils' capabilities. Individual learning is likely to vary in approach, strategy and efficiency, and exploration of itself does not always lead to success, and still less does it lead to efficient construction and solution. Given unsuccessful and unskilful efforts, further work can only result in frustration and the strengthening of poor learning rather than competence and its accompanying sense of satisfaction. Guidance is often needed and, according to the task and to the child's ability, it may vary from explicit verbal instruction to cueing the child's own exploration, and even to unaided but verbally encouraged discovery. Good teaching demands appropriate treatment based on the teacher's own judgements rather than a slavish adherence to any one approach; and there will be occasions when the teacher not only guides individual children but also gives explicit, systematic instruction to the whole class—telling, demonstrating and explaining in such a way as to make the most of his own and his pupils' language resources. He may also, when he judges it to be useful, require a whole group to engage together in rehearsal and recitation.

Reference to the pupil's language abilities raises the question of readiness to take up new learning. There is much to commend the idea of readiness if it is looked at constructively—if what is of interest is how to prepare the child for new learning—but there is a danger that it may be a very limiting concept if attention is focused on what the child is unable to do. We may delay learning because we refrain from using terms we think he may not understand, but, if understanding comes not all at once but in uncertain steps as we described in the second chapter, then it is often difficult to judge how and when a term might be grasped. Suppose we argue that a 5-year-old does not know what a sentence is and that we should therefore not use the term until he understands it. We should then deprive early readers of the use of a term that, even in its partial comprehension, is likely to be of use in classroom reading and writing activities. Moreover, by failing to identify acceptable examples of sentences we should ensure that the child was not helped to learn the term, which is a particularly difficult one in any case since its grasp requires the ability to reflect on forms of language and to analyse them. When questioning some children about sentences (Francis, 1973), I appreciated how the use of the term facilitated its grasp. Very few 5-year-olds could offer an example, nor could most of them identify a written example by distinguishing it from other symbols such as words and letters. During the following year they began to offer examples of sentences which had come from their initial reading books, and not until they were 7 did they find freedom to give examples constructed by themselves. Whether these came from direct reflection on speech or from their developing ability to write (which indirectly reflected their speech) it is difficult to say. What was clear, however, was that the concept of a sentence gained ground during early reading and was in part an outcome of developing skill, and in part an aid to the direction of further understanding. There was no such moment as a time of readiness to grasp the idea and so to use the term; but rather, as the idea grew towards its fullness so the terminology found a hold, was used more appropriately and finally settled more or less into its common usage. This is not to deny moments of sudden insight in the growth of an idea, but to point to their multiplicity and to say that we would find it hard to predict if, how and when they might occur in the case of any one child. In considering readiness to learn we should, then, take care not to hold words back from children, but rather to continue to offer them for the savouring and trying out that precedes the grasp; for with this savouring comes the mental tension of the construction of knowledge.

It has been said that discovery favours the well-prepared mind. We have just been talking about personal knowledge, but in making decisions as to what to teach we must also consider preparedness in relation to cultural experience. Can children from different backgrounds be taught similarly? As far as language is concerned, can they start from common ground with similar orientations to learn? In the last chapter we pointed to socio-cultural differences that led to different experiences of language learning, and now we have to ask whether those differences are such that children are not similarly prepared to learn.

There are writers whose answer to this question is a clear affirmative. Children are not similarly prepared to be taught, so much so that existing provision in schools is seen by many to be alien and irrelevant to their needs or interests. Midwinter (1972) is concerned that a school's instruction often fails to meet the experience of pupils in its catchment area, while Williams (1961), Young (1971) and Keddie (1971) have in their different ways explored the problems of providing schooling for children from different cultural backgrounds. Not only are questions of social control of the curriculum and various value systems discussed, but it is suggested that there are subcultural differences in receptiveness to both written and spoken means of instruction. These differences are, however, far from clear. Receptiveness to the written word, though more frequently found in middle-class children, is neither particularly well developed nor universal amongst them; while some lower working-class children develop genuinely scholarly and literary interests. If a literary subculture is to be defined it does not coincide with any subculture defined in terms of social class. Bantock (1968) was prepared to argue for different curricula to meet children's literary and academic inclinations, though how one could allocate children to appropriate schooling is a most intractable problem. It might, too, be argued that if literacy was in any sense a valued or desired state, then perhaps the aim should not be to suit apparently different children, but to encourage the arts of reading and writing in those who had not yet developed the taste. Exactly the same argument might be made about the spoken tongue, except that in this case there is a stronger tendency to see subcultures based on social class divisions and to accuse teachers of attempting to pass on a middle-class culture. This ignores the considerable differences within classes and the differences between teachers; it also implies that working-class children lack the experience and language of their middle-class age-mates —that their own is either deficient or different, and on either count ill prepares them for schooling and fails to support them through school life.

If, for the sake of examining the question of language and learning in relation to different background experiences, we allow that subcultures can be discerned, it is necessary that we consider carefully how learning might be affected. Some possible reasons for alienation do not bear on language differences, but rather on the values, motivations, intentions and abilities of the speakers. Insofar as language may be implicated, it is likely to require consideration as a variable means of encoding ideas, as a means of agreement about knowledge and as a bearer of information about different experiences. Thus alienation might arise out of unwillingness to accept a different encoding, inability to meet on common ground, or lack of understanding of what is talked about through sheer unfamiliarity.

Those who argue that cross-cultural language differences lead to differences in thinking and learning based on different ways of encoding experience draw on clear distinctions made across cultural and linguistic boundaries. Examples of more extreme variation were used by Whorf (1956) when he contrasted expressions in English with those in various American Indian tongues, and elaborated the Whorf-Sapir hypothesis that modes of thinking can be determined by the forms of language. It is certainly true that it is not always easy to translate from one language to another in that corresponding words or phrases are not available, but one hesitates to infer from this that speakers cannot share the same ideas. The metaphoric nature of many expressions within English is evidence of the powers of accommodation of the mind. Moreover, to point to lack of an expression in a language is often to point to the relative insignificance of the related experience rather than to a lack of understanding. That the Eskimo has many words for snow means that the use of different forms of snow is of more importance to him than it is to us. It does not mean that we are relatively incapable of making the distinctions because our lack of vocabulary limits us. Indeed, young lads might well appreciate some of the distinctions without the accompanying words, for the quality of snow affects the making of slides, snowballs, snowmen and the like. A more extensive vocabulary could be learned. Similarly, while different ways of expressing such features as plurality and time can be found very readily from one language to another, it would seem to be the case that these can be recognised, understood and learned.

It would seem, then, that linguistic differences are unlikely to be strong determiners of differences in thinking (and, indeed, differences seem to be relatively insignificant compared with the wide similarities to be found between languages); but it is possible that they incline speakers to respond differently to situations and thus to learning tasks. Experimental work indicates that the availability of an appropriate word facilitates remembering and recognising of the relevant aspect of an event. This is particularly evident in cross-cultural studies using colour terms, where a colour is more exactly distinguished and identified by speakers with a word for it than by those without. But, beyond this kind of term and terms in specialist areas of knowledge, it seems difficult to find examples of clear differences. If this is the case with the most marked language differences we can find, then subcultural differences are not likely to exert any very strong effect on learning. Labov (1969) warned very clearly against the assumption that contrasts between standard and non-standard American English indicated necessary differences in thinking. While not everyone would infer the speaker's thinking with the same level of confidence as did Labov, and while there may well be a statistical correlation between speech patterns and intellectual power due to some other common factor or factors, the warning cannot be dismissed. Labov further made the point that a child's command of structure in language will be shown differently in different contexts. We are reminded of our discussion of Bernstein's work on socio-linguistic differences which led to the conclusion that what differentiated children was not language difference *per se*, but different experiences of its use.

What, then, does this mean in terms of preparedness to learn? First, as long as a child stays within his socio-linguistic culture he is not likely to encounter discontinuity or misunderstanding due to different socio-linguistic experience. This is not to say that some children will not be more ready, able and willing to learn than others, for they will. Within a subculture some children's experience of language and life will be relatively deficient. When children and teachers from different backgrounds meet, however, both deficit and difference in experience may affect preparedness to learn. Differences lie in the selections of words, sentence forms and registers adopted. (Registers are forms of language deemed appropriate for use with the relevant persons and/or situations within a language community.) Nevertheless, as we have seen, different language practices may well accompany and even lead to different rates of development of particular aspects of skill. Thus difference and deficit are not mutually exclusive possibilities; they may coexist or even be interdependent. One may well argue in appropriate cases for either the compensatory education advocated by those who perceive deficit or the additional help suggested by those looking at differences, or for both.

If research into language practices in the home can be taken as a guide, some children will lack familiarity with certain kinds of verbal guidance and explanation; they may lack some concrete experiences and the concomitant vocabulary; and they may be relatively unfamiliar with more abstract concepts. They rarely, however, lack an adequate command of language for preparedness to learn. They need additional help to add to their repertoire what is judged to be needed—in particular those activities that encourage or require discussion of similarities, differences, consequences and aesthetic judgements. To prepare a curriculum based on the everyday experience of the child and on special language training in standard English which only parallels his own competence may be to deprive the relatively disadvantaged child of the verbal experience of his more fortunate counterparts by failing to take up his preparedness to expand his knowledge and trapping him within the limitations of his environment. It is worth considering how far we may call on the imagination as well as on 'reality' in educating all children, using verbal as well as pictorial and other symbolic aids to encourage and develop the imaginative extension of experience. As far as language skills are concerned, there is much to be said for Lawton's (1975) argument for a common culture curriculum which allows for individual differences, rather than different curricula designed for ill-defined social groups. Questions of interest, skill, value and relevance can be explored within such a framework rather than be grounds for differentiating between curricula.

Lawton argues that such a curriculum would be primarily concerned with experience within generally publicly agreed forms of knowledge which represent common cultural concerns rather than subcultural differences. These are thought of as disciplines which define not only the content but also the ways of going about activities within them. Arguing that selections of available disciplines could provide common ground for all pupils, giving good coverage and balance within the culture, Lawton suggests five broad disciplines—mathematics, natural sciences, humanities and social sciences, expressive and creative arts, and moral education. We have no grounds for thinking that subcultural language differences justify different emphases within this broad division. All versions of English (not to mention other tongues) as spoken within society draw on experience across all these disciplines. Lawton agrees that the divisions are arguable, but effectively claims that alternatives do not violate the notion of a common culture and a common curriculum. In fact, when the illustrations of how it might be put into practice are given, it appears that disciplines often break down in practical and theoretical terms into fairly traditional 'subject' areas. The main strength of the approach is that while extending possibilities for pupils of lower ability and for those who have been traditionally denied access to the kinds of learning incorporated in the grammar school curriculum, it also suggests reassessment of some of the attitudes and practices within that tradition. Here Lawton's considerations do seem to rest on certain views of the nature of knowledge and learning that are in accord with those that we have been building in the course of our examination of the place of language in learning.

We have, however, tended to emphasise cognitive learning, and perhaps it is time to examine Jones's (1968) criticisms of some of the American work on new curricula, arising in particular out of his looking at some of Bruner's enthusiastic developments. Jones points out that unless children's feelings and imaginings are engaged in new learning much meaning is passed by or lost, and learning tends to become rather arid. The illustrations he gives show that language can be used to express and reflect upon feelings aroused by new experiences in learning, and can both enhance understanding and free the thinking of the child. Jones was particularly interested in observing how children reacted to a course of instruction about the Netsilik Eskimo. This particular course was part of a bigger programme with the aim of fostering a better understanding of the nature of man. The materials used included specially produced film, and were so good that the children responded with strong emotion as well as thoughtful perception; but the teachers were unprepared to deal with anxiety and with anger and revulsion as a means to a better understanding of the ways of mankind. Consequently there was a tendency for the children to act out scenes of death and hunting and killing in their dance lessons, an outcome that both worried and bored the dancing instructress. The children also tended to treat the topics rather dismissively in their written work, saying things to the effect that they have their ways and we have ours. They also tended to draw up summary lists of culture contrasts without any evidence of much awareness of their meanings. Yet there was one teacher who somehow managed both to allow and to encourage children to talk about their reactions pretty fully and frankly; and they then went on to consider why the Netsilik acted as they did with respect to babies and old folk who could not be supported by the group, and to the seal they had to hunt for food, fuel and clothing. The children were able to think about the ways the Netsilik coped with their emotions in their way of life. The following extracts illustrate something of what happened when the children had learned that babies were sometimes abandoned:

Pupils' comments: It's mean. They're cruel. The baby has a right to live. Don't they have any feelings? Does it hurt to freeze? Why do they live there?
Teacher: When I first heard about this custom that the Netsilik have, I almost had a sick feeling much like you had: 'It's mean, it's cruel, it's stupid.' Then I found out something else that made a difference. The

Netsilik don't really like to abandon babies, but they believe a baby has no soul until it has a name. So what might they do to help their feelings out?
Pupils' comments: Not name the baby if they're going to abandon it. Then they're not murderers. (Jones, 1968, p. 39)

These 10-year-old children were able from this point to compare beliefs and practices in American society with those of the Netsilik in ways that threw more understanding on both, so that the aim of understanding mankind was more closely approached.

In an essay elsewhere Jones (1966) refers to the way writings in the psychoanalytic tradition have drawn our attention to the manner in which our conscious thoughts are influenced by the links they have with memories and their associated emotions. Creative thinking is not just the association and transformation of ideas exercised in consciousness, but is dependent on the connections and relations made in pre-conscious thought—thought that lies just below the surface of our awareness. Words and ideas come to our minds not entirely as we intentionally dig them out, but as if we offer them to ourselves or are impelled to accept them. Jones illustrates the way the pre-conscious can be tapped to enhance children's writing by using observations of 7-year-old children's work with a particular teacher. Her aim was for the children to write short poems using personification in their writing. She had given them some illustrative examples, but the children's own first attempts failed to be more than rhyming description. Then the teacher, using another illustration, explained how the poet had used his imagination. Taking the children's ideas of imagination as *not real* or *pictures in the head*, she encouraged them to lay down their heads and let something come to mind, and then to try to think what it reminded them of. They then drew pictures and wrote sentences to develop and record their imaginings and analogies. After this experience they tried again to write poems, and this time some of them achieved the desired end. The following is an example.

> Look at the sun running
> I think I know why it is running so fast
> It is running to the next day
> And then it will come back to us. (Jones 1966, p. 10)

For Jones, no significant new learning is simply the receipt of facts, however well organised, or of principles, however well presented. Nor is it only an act of cognitive construction on the part of the child, though it must include that. It is, rather, the active projection of the self on to what is to be learned—thoughtful and emotional construction bound inextricably with life experience. If we take the same view we must see the language of education as that which ideally promotes in each child the fullest possible use of language in accord with his developing personality.

5

Language in the Classroom

Having discussed aspects of the use of language in teaching and learning we will now set them in the context of actual formal educational conditions where the language of the social structure of the school and classroom both envelops and sustains efforts to instruct. We shall first illustrate something of what is meant by the enveloping language with reference to the transition from home to school, and then look at examples of classroom teaching.

In the new learning context of school, the child finds new social relationships and new persons to guide and share his achievements. The transition is not only made when he first attends—it happens every day of his school life. Now we have already seen that the language of instruction in the home seems to vary between homes and between different subgroups of the population, and that the social structure and values of the families and groups are important determiners of the selection of ways of speaking, so we are prepared to consider similar differences between homes and schools. These are not so much differences of social class (as those who criticise schools for middle-class values would have us believe) but rather differences between home and school institutions. Many teachers of working-class origin support the customs and language of the school where they teach, and 40 per cent of teachers come from such a background (Morrison and McIntyre, 1973). Also many working-class parents support them, and the ways of schools bear analysis in their own right. It may not be the case, as Bernstein and Henderson (1969) seem to assume, that the schools' ways of instruction encourage autonomy in the sphere of skills, and reflexiveness in the interpersonal, but it may be that some schools' ways do while others' do not. Disharmony between home and school contexts of learning may be the experience of a child from any social background.

Some of the important language customs of both homes and schools centre on modes of address and on the forms used to establish and maintain the social structure of the institution and the nature of the teaching-learning contract. We often see this as being more true of the school than of the home. We are inclined to think that young children at home will accept guidance with only relatively minor objections and that only older children and adolescents are likely to bargain and to challenge ways of talking. But this is to fail to appreciate the extent of the agreement laid down in infancy and constantly worked upon by mother and child. Learning how to talk to each other and how to agree on what is to be done is a long-drawn-out process, biased in favour of the social practices valued by the mother, whether of her personal choice or her social allegiance, though it is by no means entirely determined by her. It is also biased as an adult-child and expert-novice contract, rather than as one between social and knowledgeable equals. When the child enters into a learning situation with another instructor he does so with the expectations learned in these early years. As long as they are not violated too much he will be inclined to co-operate, and he will probably tolerate some considerable differences until he has had time to weigh them up. Otherwise he will carry his expectancies with him and possibly cross those of his new instructor's. In general he is likely to expect intuitively that the nature of what is to be learned will increase his autonomy and skill and that his learning will meet with the kind of reward or punishment, approval or disapproval, to which he is accustomed. He may also be well-disposed to further learning, though he may treat his own choice as being more interesting than what the instructor attempts to present. Interest depends on what the child can and wants to make his own in a very personal way. If, however, no satisfactory contract, however implicit, is worked out, there will be increasing alienation and conflict—such as can be seen in some adolescents in schools. Moreover, by adolescence it is evident that the power-relations in the home and, indeed, in the world at large are shifting from the marked adult-child bias of early childhood through that uneasy transition towards a more adult-adult relationship.

What, we may ask, are the language practices that feed the contractual situation, and how do they change from home to school? One is the form of address. The mother-child contract usually conveys the status difference with a title, *Mother* or *Mum*, versus a personal name or a term conveying both emotion and address to a small child, such as *dear* or *rascal*. The emotional overtones convey something of the intimacy of a family relationship and neither the label nor the overtones can be used by another, less intimate, instructor. Thus the transition is made by the child from addressing a parent to addressing an unrelated adult with some such form as *Miss, Sir,* or *Miss Smith*. Paralleling this shift will be a pronoun shift in some languages as in the French *tu* to *vous*. In English there is no change in *you* but the overtones of the use of the word shift from the more intimate to the more impersonal. On the surface this shift may seem a trivial matter of simply learning the appropriate forms, but if we consider that in making the change the child is entering a situation with no worked out learning contract and is permitting a stranger to act *in loco parentis* we see that it signifies more than at first appears. We also see how easy it might be for the unwitting or insensitive teacher to fail to grasp the implications and expect the child simply to conform to alien expectations, failing to appreciate that forms of address are associated with a whole range of ways of talking and controlling behaviour.

A few examples of the range of differences in secondary schools can be used to illustrate this point. In one context, while the master is addressed as *Sir*, and the head as *Headmaster*, the pupil is called by his surname and in some situations is even himself addressed as *Sir*, as when he has been acting in a manner contrary to that understood to be mature! Yet even this is not intended to detract from, but rather to emphasise, the understanding that both pupils and masters are 'gentlemen'. The whole style of conversation is geared to the aim of fitting the pupils for the status and ways of life of the parents who pay for their education, and is part of a system of school rules about behaviour that are more or less effective in relation to the kind of contract to which teachers, parents and pupils subscribe in large measure. Something of this kind of agreement and something of the associated social context with its complex of rules, both written and unwritten, characterised the grammar schools until the post-1944 era, and to some extent have done so in even more recent years. But since 1944 these schools have seen changes related to those in the whole social structure. More pupils have aimed for higher education before finding their adult employment, so that the schools have carried an even stronger academic orientation; while at the same time they have admitted proportionately more pupils who find this emphasis uncongenial, and who have no footing in the ways of life related to the older type of school and which are even now carried over to some extent into the newer. There is, then, an absence of a suitably worked out contract with these pupils, in spite of recent concern with curriculum research and innovation, and simply looking to adaptation of the curriculum is not a sufficient approach to their being positively involved in their schooling. Now that more than half of our upper schools are comprehensive the question of forging learning contracts is acute, and the language of discipline and indiscipline reflects the problems.

The post-war secondary modern schools were often characterised by the social structure inherited from the old senior elementary schools, where the school leaving age of 14 meant that no serious accommodation to the needs of adolescents was required; and the language of pupil-teacher relationships fitted the obedience and authority expected in the junior schools and in many of the work situations which awaited the pupils on leaving school. By the 1960s, however, many schools had seen considerable change in this respect, and some carried pupils on to take O level examinations. They rarely, however, aped the older grammar schools in their social rules, but were sometimes influenced by the new, with their emphasis on academic attainment, especially when such schools were the kind the teachers themselves had experienced in adolescence. The forms of address had no hangover of gentlemanly implications, even when the pupil was called *Jones* rather than *Tom*. A high proportion of pupils, however, expected to take up occupations that did not require academic or even other skilled qualifications, and the unwritten contract was a kind of tolerant sitting-it-out until leaving school was allowed. When the school leaving age rose, and as parents seemed to place less value on schooling, many of these pupils came to express towards their teachers and schools the challenge to authority that was more evident in society at large. More pupils, then, could be found in the kind of anti-school culture described by Hargreaves (1967) in a secondary modern school and by Lacey (1970) in a grammar school, and this has continued to show itself in many of the new comprehensives. Francis (1975), who taught in such schools and recognised that the problem of classroom control was of paramount importance for probationary teachers in such contexts, illustrated the language of the power conflict that occurs when no learning agreement has been forged. When not pushed the teacher addressed his pupils by their first names, but when angry he switched to surnames. *Terry. Come here and pick up these books* was followed, after Terry Benton's delay, by *Benton, pick up these books and place them on my desk*. The pupils tended to address him routinely as *Sir*, but frequently omitted any name; yet when they became insolent, or combined to annoy him, they used a nickname or an over-emphasised *Sir*.

But the actual form of address is only a part of the language of the social context of school instruction. The forms of verbal control are many and varied. They operate in a wide framework of control via the physical structure of buildings, the social structure of the teaching staff, the explicit and implicit rules of behaviour, and the non-verbal means of interpersonal control. From nursery to sixth form, these ways of expressing what may go on set the scene for teaching and so define the kinds of communication that teacher and pupil are expected to use in the guidance of learning.

An important feature of address in schools is that groups of children are often the object. At home and outside school this is a much less frequent experience, but when each teacher has a class of twenty to thirty pupils, and when some occasions and some teaching techniques require that the class is addressed as a whole, talking to a group rather than individuals is inevitable. In addition to the formal groups arranged by the teachers, there are also the informal groupings which are made by the pupils themselves and which are not congruent with the formal. These have their own values and ways of behaving that may or may not correspond with those desired of them by the school. Sometimes their cohesion is only occasionally expressed in opposition to teachers or to other groups, as when children who normally work and behave in line with the teacher's expectations show opposition on a particular issue. But when groups are constantly acting against the teaching, and when formal classes are not learning or behaving as desired, then the opposition is often expressed on both sides in ways that include verbal attack and derogatory labelling. This tends to harden and confirm the lack of agreement and to define a situation in which learning has not only been relatively poor in the past but is unlikely to develop satisfactorily thereafter. This is particularly true of the adolescent stage of learning, but conflict can also be seen in primary schools in those situations where a teacher or another group of pupils defines one group as dull or badly behaved. Unfortunately for any child associated with such a group, even if only by formal allocation to it rather than any sense of belonging, all members are branded in the same way. Stereotyping, a shorthand way of defining a group, can be costly in human terms.

The formal organisation of a school may exacerbate the expression of such definitions. Hargreaves selected instances of remarks made by both teachers and pupils in a streamed secondary school—remarks which can illustrate stereotyping based in part on the streaming:

Teaching to A stream: We like to think the A stream have more common sense than the rest. Do you want to let us down?

Teacher to B stream making a noise in the corridor: Who are you lot?
Boys: 3B, Sir.
Teacher: You sound more like 1E than 3B.

Teacher to 4B: This is 4B. You wouldn't believe that this was next to the top class. Does B stand for blockheads? (Hargreaves, 1967, p. 95)

Such remarks may sometimes be thought by teachers to be relatively harmless, but constant exposure to them may encourage the attitudes expressed below by boys:

A and B streams speaking about C and D streams: They're scruffy. They get good clothes but they don't look after them. They think they're tough. A few of them are all right in 4C. A lot of them are big-headed, you know, walking around beating kids up and smoking. They all look dumb. I'd rather be at the bottom of the top class than at the top of the bottom class. (ibid., p. 73)

C and D streams speaking about A and B streams: They're all daft. Toffee-noses. You know, snobs. They think they're clever. Just 'cos they're in a higher class than us they think they're better than us. They're teachers' pets. They're mad that lot. They're staying on most of them. (ibid., p. 75)

That these stereotypes carry some weight is seen in the problems of pupils who were moved from a B stream to an A stream:

Newcomer to A stream: At first a lot wouldn't bother with us. We got the usual fools who started making wise-cracks. Saying things about your face and that. But this is serious. They mean it. It's not just a joke. (ibid., p. 21)

A stream members about newcomers: We're not really keen on the lads who've come up. The old 3A's still there really. Well, Adrian and us sort of shut them out, you know what I mean? It'll be smashing next year, 'cos there aren't many of the lads who came up staying on. You know, it's the original 3A who're staying on. (ibid., p. 16)

These quotations have pointed to many aspects of interpersonal relations within classrooms and schools and of learning contexts. Into these different environments with different approaches to instruction come children from the different experiences of learning, of control and of family relationships which we discussed in chapter 3. The teacher obviously takes up his or her own preferred means of conducting affairs in the classroom whether or not they are congruent with those of the home, and the effects can be seen in ways of instructing and in techniques of control. What is a 5-year-old to make, for example, of a teacher's insistence that he answer questions differently from his usual manner? *Where is your reading book?* is likely to be answered by *In my locker* rather than *My book is in my locker, Miss*, but it is not unusual for the latter kind of answer to be required by a teacher who has been led to think she is thus fostering language development. If a young child expects control via short commands, hugs and slaps, he may not realise the implications of *John, why are you playing with Peter?*, when the teacher is suggesting he should be carrying on with some other activity. Instead of returning to the teacher-preferred behaviour as he might if told *John, get on with your reading* or if physically guided back to it, he is likely to answer with something like *Because he's made a good plane, Miss*. Another child, accustomed to more subtle verbal control, is more likely to return to his book; but he, on the other hand, is likely to find a slap or physical control less comprehensible in the context. Unless such differences are appreciated the behaviour of the child who does not do what the teacher expects is judged unfavourably, and the learning situation may be defined to the child as inexplicably punishing. For the child who does conform to expectations, however, it can be rewarding unless his conformity arouses the antagonism of his peers.

Facing a network of possible pupil reactions in a complex classroom situation, the teacher attempts to arrange matters so that her pupils learn within some syllabus she can specify. This may be determined by other agents such as more senior teachers or examining bodies and may be embedded in a wider explicitly defined curriculum (it is always embedded in whatever unspecified assumptions and values lie behind the teaching) or it may be broadly defined by joint agreement with pupils and worked out in the light of the teacher's greater knowledge, competence and access to useful materials. Where external examinations are to be willingly taken, then the teacher and pupils must accept some of the syllabus constraints, for part of the learning contract is an agreement to work for examination success. Apart from this, however, the syllabus is likely to arise from what is thought within the school to be appropriate for the age, sex and abilities of the pupils concerned. Acknowledging that decisions may be arguable, ill-informed, and based on prejudice, we shall continue in this chapter to look at the use of language in the classroom at different age levels, bearing in mind that the children are not only learning in greater or lesser degree what the teacher is aiming for, but are also learning how to protect their interests and even to survive in the classroom settings in which lessons take place.

Let us first take the pre-school level—doing so because so much emphasis has recently been placed on language training for disadvantaged children; and also because the 4- to 5-year-olds do not form strong subgroups and the total class size is likely to be smaller than that for other age levels. The possibilities of creating a learning environment free from power and value conflict should be maximal. Examples of verbal exchange in nursery education can be gleaned from such language training programmes as those of Bereiter and Engelmann (1966) and Marion Blank (1968). The approaches are slightly different, Bereiter and Engelmann aiming to teach the children to speak standard English (almost as a second language) while Blank aims to promote abstract thinking. In the former case the child is deemed to lack an appropriate language while in the latter he is seen not to be using his language as usefully as he might. Bereiter and Engelmann therefore have the teacher provide examples of statements that correspond with some evident state of affairs, and contrasting statements to correspond with an alternative situation. The children are expected to repeat these statements and practise them well, so techniques such as rhythmic repetition and chanting in unison are adopted. The teacher has to command attention and act as a sort of cheer leader. A short extract from one transcription can illustrate the technique:

Teacher: This is a _____.
Child: Gun.
Teacher: Good. It is a gun.
Let's all say it.
This is a gun. This is a gun.
Again. This is a gun.
Let's say it one more time. This is an alligator.
Child: It ain't neither. It a gun. (Bereiter and Engelmann, 1966, p. 105)

Here we can see something very like programmed instruction. A small step, reinforcement with approval and confirmation, and then repetition of response. We can also see the deliberate use of a contrast statement, not congruent with evidence, which fulfilled a primary purpose of gaining the sagging attention of the children who had been chanting with the teacher, but which also satisfied the logic of the programme. But what happened? Neither at the end of the exchange nor at any other point in the transcription did a child freely use a statement with *It is* or *This is*. While taking one instance may be an unfair criticism of the effectiveness of the technique, the contrast between accurate imitation and spontaneous production may imply that far from understanding the relationship between the repeated statement and the state of affairs for which it was a 'mapping' the child was not making a mental interpretation of the full statement. He was not engaged in a contract to try to learn but simply to do what the teacher said. Perhaps much of the child's language in school is like this—conforming, rather than informing the teacher about his learning. This is a disturbing thought, but if most young children on entering school manage the unfamiliar new context by trying to conform to what they perceive as requirements, rather than by entering into a learning dialogue with the teacher, then the very foundation of formal education would seem to be problematic.

We can, however, find examples of children's language which are less open to doubt. In attempting to encourage language and thinking, Blank recommends engaging in dialogue over some purposeful activity chosen by the child. The child's remarks tend to be shorter than the teacher's, but they are generally spontaneous and related closely to monitoring or choosing activities. By encouraging plenty of conversation the teacher tests the child's vocabulary and provides new concepts in the course of play. Efforts are made to encourage talking about remembered events and commenting on features of ongoing activity, including the talking itself. In such dialogue the child does seem more interested than in the group practice activities of the Bereiter and Engelmann extract, and is informing the teacher much more fully about his or her understanding and ability. There does seem to be about this kind of context something of the informal contract of the mother-child situation at home, although the teacher's objectives and practices are more developed and explicit than those of most mothers. Even in this situation, however, we can see evidence of misunderstanding, as the following extract from a transcript suggests:

Teacher: See I got some things ready for you. Do you remember what you wanted to do today with these things?
Lisa: Give a bath.
Teacher: Right, that's just what you asked for yesterday. Okay, now how should we do it?
Lisa: Give her a bottle, then she sleep. (Blank, 1973)

Blank saw this last as an inappropriate 'rote' response, by which she seemed to mean it to be an unconsidered, frequently used remark. The teacher wanted the child to describe the process of giving the doll a bath, but before we judge the child's remark to be inappropriate perhaps we ought to ask how she understood the teacher's question. We cannot know an answer to this, of course, but it is quite possible that the question was given a different meaning by the child because the whole bath process was, in her experience of babies, a total bathing and feeding sequence. If this were so, then the episode would be a good example of the way misunderstanding can arise from assumptions about shared knowledge when in fact both parties are bringing different prior knowledge to the transaction. The extent to which the first of the child's schoolteachers manage to bridge the gap between the mutual understanding of mother and child and the lack of any such shared experience between themselves and the child is probably very significant in relation to the youngster's confidence in schooling and his expectations of teachers' behaviour. He does not want a surrogate parent, but he does need a teacher who can build with him on his existing knowledge and ways of doing things. He needs to feel he can control and predict events sufficiently to avoid helplessness; otherwise it is possible for the transition to school to lead to a slowing down of everyday learning and a specialisation into relatively limited instructional settings. In a fairly large class of schoolchildren each also has to learn how to cope best with the new environment, the new teacher, and new age-mates. While transition to school is well recognised as a time of adjustment it is possible that the full extent of the demands made on children is not readily appreciated; nor is it perhaps remembered that a related daily transition takes place throughout school life.

In the examples discussed above, teachers were concentrating on language learning; but instruction is also directed towards social, physical, artistic and cognitive skills. The teacher may use a variety of instructional methods, sometimes attending to a whole class together, sometimes helping an individual child, and sometimes monitoring and guiding group activities and discussion. An example of classroom language (Rosen and Rosen 1973, p. 46) is to be used as an illustration of what can be involved when a teacher encourages a class of 6-year-olds to talk. Social skill in verbal exchange, comprehension and the construction of remarks are interwoven and fostered together. In the selected extract the teacher aimed to introduce a theme and encourage ways of exploring it in a form of guided verbal discovery. She modelled the kind of exploration she had in mind, and tried to keep the children to the theme. In this case it was the observation of the building of a bird's nest under the school roof and of subsequent happenings in the nest:

Teacher: I've something to tell you. Mr Jackson found the shell of one broken egg on the ground the other day. And he thought, 'There's one baby bird, because here's the shell that's broken now. The baby's come out of the shell.' Mr Jackson thought there was only one baby bird, but really there are _____?
Pupil: Three.
Teacher: Three babies. How do you know there are three?
Pupil: Because I saw all their heads pop up.
Teacher: What did we see yesterday?
Pupil: All their heads popped up. And they all made a noise. And they all went ... and two went down. No. One went down and ... they both, they stayed up.... And for a little while they both popped down again.
Teacher: And when they popped their heads up, what did they do? Can you tell us about it, Gary?
Gary: When I was at home, I saw this egg. And it was broken. And there was a little baby bird laying there dead.
Teacher: Yes. Sometimes they fall out of the nest, don't they?
Pupil: What?
Gary: The egg was broken.
Pupil: What happened?
Gary: The egg was broken. It must have been the bird was out. And he fell on the ground and was dead.
Second pupil: It must have been cracking open. It must have rolled over and he must have fell.
Third pupil: I know. A cat must have had it.
Teacher: Who else has got something to tell us about our bird? Lise?
Lise: When I was going out in my garden, I went on this slide and ... and this ... I was going down the slope. And I heard birds whistling. And I looked on the seat where you sit to slide down ... and I saw a bird's nest. It had six eggs in it 'cos it was a great big one ... and I saw a bird sitting on 'em.

Certain points are worth comment. Several pupils engaged in the exchange, and the teacher, monitoring the activities, drew in first Gary and then Lise. The latter had said little but was obviously able to make some contribution. There was, however, no language of behavioural management, except monitoring of ideas in the direct exchange of questions, answers and comments in the discussion. The participants were free to talk, not distracted by alternative behaviour of any of their members or of other pupils. This was, then, a promising situation for learning. It was, moreover, one in which the total pupil talk also outweighed the teacher's and some of the pupils' remarks were quite long. Now what happened? Overall the teacher managed to keep the children thinking about birds and nests, and Rosen reports that this was regarded by other teachers as well done. Nevertheless, the model of inquiry set up by the teacher, using *because* structures, was not taken up readily by the children except in direct response to a *How do you know ... ?* question. *'Cos* was used naturally, but not apparently logically, in *It had six eggs in it 'cos it was a great big one.* The children preferred to talk about their observations in a more narrative style, but this did sometimes suggest relationships in their thinking which were partially in line with the teacher's aims. And in further extracts Rosen shows how the teacher produced more modelling and more questions to elicit the kind of thought she was encouraging. It is important to appreciate the discrepancies between desired and actual performance, and the way these both informed the teacher of the pupils's abilities and interest and set up in at least some of the children a productive tension—a tendency to take up the modelling.

Another use of language in the first school classroom is the verbal exchange between pupils engaged in some constructive, artistic or problem-solving activity. One can see not only that the activity is of interest, but that the conversation is itself an artistic construction on the part of the children, attempting to solve something of the problem of the interpersonal exchange of ideas. Piaget (1959) saw true dialogue as being of great importance in the child's learning, implying as it does the ability to take up something of another's point of view which may constitute a challenge to one's own thinking. This is different from the challenge of the probably unquestioned authority of the adult in the pupil-teacher relationship in the primary school. It is important to note that if Piaget's interpretations are correct then such dialogue does not readily occur before children are about 7, for at younger ages viewpoints are too egocentric. Unlike the older child or adult retelling a narrative, and reconstructing it and shortening it but retaining order and meaning, the under-7 child selects points that catch his interest and retells them without due regard for the whole story or for the hearer's understanding. Yet he is often quite astonished at his listener's lack of comprehension. A similar communication failure is evident in explanations of mechanical drawings, when, although the child gives independent evidence of understanding the adult's prior explanation, he cannot express this account to another child. He omits to name important features, and one is reminded of the dependence on pronouns in referring to pictures which we have already noted when discussing socio-linguistic codes. What was there related to notions of a restricted code is described by Piaget in developmental terms:

'Finally, one of the facts which point most definitely to the ego-centric character of the explanations of children is the large proportion of cases in which the explainer completely forgets to name the objects which he is explaining, as in the case of taps and syringes. This holds good for half of the explainers from 6 to 7, and for one-sixth of those between 7 and 8. They assume that their hearer will understand from the outset what they are talking about. Naturally, in such cases, the reproducer gives up trying to understand, and repeats the explanation he has received, without attempting to assign a name to the object in question.' (Piaget, 1959, p. 107)

In the light of these observations we should obviously ask ourselves, when young children are talking to each other in groups, just how, and how well, one child can help another at the age in question.

When we turn from the primary school stages to examine language in the classroom in middle and upper schools, we find that teaching and learning nest more evidently in ways of managing the class and the learning. Transcripts of lessons reveal the teacher's concern with controlling pupils' behaviour in order to create conditions for learning. There is less freedom for the pupil to move about the room and to follow personal interests than there is for children in first schools and there is more clearly defined group and class teaching, and consequently organisation and management language is a feature of teacher-class relationships rather than of teacher-pupil exchange. The resulting tension between teachers' and pupils' corporate aims to control the class and the individual pupil's need for personal communication produces many minor disruptive incidents. Examples can be seen in the following transcript from a lesson with children about eight years old (Moseley and Hamblin, 1972, p. 45):

Teacher: Before noon it is ante-meridian, or a.m. If it's after, it's post-meridian. What does that mean? Can you guess, post-meridian? Yes, Simon?
Child: Afternoon.
Teacher: Afternoon. That's right. Good boy.

So far so good. The teacher is heading the way she wants to go and a co-operative child has supplied the correct answer to her question. The teacher-class context produces a style of instruction not unlike programmed learning in spite of the interpersonal potential. But next comes a deviant move in the game when another pupil speaks.

Child: It's like when somebody's having a baby: it's post-mature if it's after ...

Now the teacher is distracted and attends to the use of *post-mature*, interrupting the child's possible completion of her illustration and thereby not taking up a check on her understanding. Instead she corrects her.

Teacher: It's post-natal and ante-natal, not mature.
Child: I know, but ...

Here the child has moved into the interpersonal style which cannot be allowed to continue if the rest of the class is not to be lost, so the teacher cuts her short and returns to the point.

Teacher: That's right. Good girl. Yes, post, good.
Child: My mummy told me about the p.m. and the a.m. and I worked it out. In the mornings it's a.m. and if it's in the afternoon it's p.m.
Teacher: Good. Well I want you to practise doing it with these cards that I've made you.

Here one feels that the teacher has been switched off course by one child's evident grasp of the distinction to be taught, and has not adequately checked the learning of other pupils. Instead she introduces another section of the lesson—activity with the cards she has made. That she becomes aware of this is evident by a return to the explanation, but not before interruptions have set in.

Teacher: Alright, shush the rest of you! If you want to get bottle tops to draw round for clocks then do so. Could you just get on quietly for a minute, Anna? Just a minute Donald please. Any time after 12 o'clock at night, midnight, until 12 o'clock, noon (which is our lunch-time isn't it?) we say ante-meridian, or a.m.

This illustrates the mix of language for the plea for quiet, for direction of activity and for explanation of ideas. We may notice that the language of management is more concise and simply expressed than that of explanation. The latter tends to become involved and to deviate from grammatical acceptability. Nevertheless, it may be the case that spoken explanations are sometimes clearer with an ordering that would be less acceptable in written accounts. Perhaps more important than the question of form is that of timing and emphasis, and in the last remark above we may be left wondering how many of the pupils attended to it when it followed so closely a mixture of multidirectional management utterances.

It is clear from the illustration we have used, and from its continuation which we will not pursue here, that class teaching tends to induce an instructional style like programmed learning, and also tends to bias the opportunity to speak away from the pupils and towards the teacher. Not only does she say more than any one pupil—she says more than the whole class put together. This is far from unusual, as analyses of classroom talking based on Flanders's techniques of analysis have shown. Flanders (1970) claimed that two-thirds of each lesson is taken up with talk, and that two-thirds of the talk is the teacher's. The net effect is to set up a context wherein pupils have to learn the permitted modes of speaking and possibly to conform to a regime that suggests that the approved answer—short and in line with the teacher's direction—is more important than the question or answer that seeks or expresses ways of understanding. It would seem that if a pupil is to be able to talk, then both he and the teacher should be able to count on co-operation from other pupils. Without this basic classroom discipline communication for learning breaks down. We are back again to the question of a learning contract, and it is clear that as children leave their first schools it becomes more important to make the agreement explicit. Older children will ask more questions about the purposes of lessons, their relevance to themselves, and freedom of choice in learning. They are also concerned with each other's aims and needs as well as their own and the teacher's. Before we treat the question of language and the content of learning within the intended syllabus for older children, we shall spend a little time considering in more detail the language of classroom control.

This is essentially a language of the definition and balance of power, and it cannot be treated in terms of a naive view of discipline as the exercise of the teacher's authority and the use of sanctions to see that rules are kept. In subtle and more obvious ways older pupils show that they, too, command the situation. They can respond to the teacher's behaviour with activities from a spectrum of possibilities, from co-operation through compliance and conformity to outright rejection. Otty (1972), in describing incidents in his early teaching, includes mention of an occasion when he could not prevent the class talking loudly, and when suddenly, apparently without leadership, the noise abated and the class began writing, talking only in whispers. He had been ignored; the class had taken control. He also quoted instances of the use of somewhat abusive shouting by teachers to which pupils responded with sullen compliance. Often the adolescent is only allowing a teacher to get on with the job, rather than co-operating in learning, and is either conforming out of habit or else complying, while saying in his heart what he really thinks about the schooling. Under these conditions discipline is far from being a static ideal condition—it is something to be constructed out of daily meeting to some agreed purpose. The teacher has the extremely difficult job of persuading pupils who are compelled to attend, and to experience the contraints of institutional life, that something worthwhile can be forged even in such unpromising conditions. Indeed he may sometimes himself need to be so persuaded by his pupils!

When the teacher is involved in guiding group or class activities the power-relations which influence speaking and what is spoken are not at all easy to define and understand. Moreover, with the same teacher and the same class, they will shift from day to day; while the differences between any two classes of similar ability doing the same kind of work can be so great that the teacher's approach to the two is obviously not the same—a fact that contributes to even greater differences. It is often noticeable, too, that the more conspicuous pupils vary from one class to another, and are not always the powerful but rather the mediators of power. Bright and alert children will only make a spoken, public, contribution when they feel their position in the group is not thereby threatened, while foolishness is not shown where peers will not support it. In a class which throws up a noisy clown others may be using that pupil to avoid exposure of their own potential folly. Pupils who support the vocal, able child may be approving ability but sheltering from exposing their own possible weaknesses. In a class where some are noisy disrupters, other pupils are supporting the aim of not working without showing their own commitment to that aim. The teacher's sarcasm, approval or punishment often serves to reinforce the pupils' power to the extent of exacerbating the problems of the children whose speaking exposes them to the public gaze. Such pupils are often far from being happy in their position. How can instruction be attempted in such contexts, let alone be effective, unless the teacher comes to know his pupils and positively to require behaviour that allows his intentions to be carried out—that sets the scene for the possibility of learning something more than how to survive? There is no set formula for how he should exercise control, but his physical, mental and personal resources will often be fully stretched; and without the alertness and 'withitness' described by Kounin (1970) the management of pupils' activities will fall short of the goal of setting the scene for learning.

Consider the language in the following description of a class out of control, and note the comments which reflect the group structure of the class and its potential for power games. The class took five minutes to enter the room and choose their seats, all the while clattering, banging and arguing their way. Then a series of management exchanges began, including the following (Francis, 1975, pp. 18-19):

— Sir?
— Yes, Jenny?
— Please, sir, Norma's in my place, sir.
— No, I ain't. (Norma, hard as nails and twice as spiky, clearly wasn't in the mood to move. Mr Jenkins chose discretion.)
— Yes, well ... there's a place over there.
— She's not coming here! (scandalised yell from Ken, whose mates found it briefly funny, and threw in congratulations, whistles and obscene suggestions.)
— She's not sitting wi' us, sir.
— But that's my place, sir, where Norma is.
— Jenny will you please sit down there. (Quiet and uncomplaining, she went, as he'd known she would. Perhaps travelling around for eight lessons a day with Norma Lewis, you got used to giving in. Still, *ten minutes gone* and nothing happening....)

How much time is taken up in how many lessons by such exchanges?

Sometimes, however, the battle rages over the actual attempts to teach. Groans greet the start of the lesson or a change of activity, accompanied by remarks such as *Do we have to do this?, What's the point?, Why do they expect us to learn about this?, It's rubbish*, and inevitably also by diversionary strategies such as *I haven't got a pencil, You didn't give me my book back, Sir*, or *I can't see the blackboard*. These are the more polite versions of the range of remarks pupils produce, but the message is clear: *Don't tell us—persuade us, or let's do something different*. And it's no use expecting the teacher miraculously to tap hypothetical pupil interests. He needs to go beyond that and sell wares whose quality he is sure of, and for whose worth he can argue. Interest has sometimes to be created. Time, thought and energy are needed in using language that insists on the pupils giving the learning an honest chance and displays wares from which they can make a genuine acceptance or rejection. When one pupil, whose resistance had been obvious, once asked, *How do you know what you know?*, and the teacher asked why she wanted to know, the answer came: *You know so much it gets interesting*. The implications of this from a semi-literate teenager whose educational diet may well have been of scant and superficial knowledge are worth examining. It was an open request to be asked into another world of experience. A learning contract was being forged, and even for those pupils who had not found such a door opening for them, the lessons thereafter took on a new quality of peace and engagement.

In contrast, what is to be made of an exchange reported by Otty (1972), p. 65) in which lower sixth form pupils responded apathetically to some orchestral pieces (presented because they differed from both 'classical' and 'pop' categories) and showed no interest in further music whether provided by teacher or pupil? The exchange is interpreted by Otty as an indication of the pupils' defensiveness against being thought anti-intellectual or philistine, or possibly from the wrong background. But there may be a further point. Did the teacher know, and value, what he wanted to do? Only if the teacher exposes his knowledge and values will the pupils have sufficient reference points—and therefore confidence —to reject, to offer or to ask for more.

Nesting within the language of management of learning contexts are problems of the language of different subject areas of the curriculum. Again we can only use examples to illustrate some important difficulties, but all subjects require the pupils' understanding of new concepts. In the second chapter we looked at relevant aspects of language development, but we are now asking how the comprehension and expression of new ideas are attempted in the classroom. In one observation of a science lesson with 10-year-olds the teacher was trying to deal with the concept of *energy*. He spent some time talking about his own and the pupils' daily eating habits, and then asked the class the purpose of eating food. Eliciting the reply that it was to preserve strength, the teacher proceeded to ask why one should wish to be strong. At this stage in the lesson no one knew where the teacher was heading, but one pupil made a trial move. His reply was not what the teacher wanted, but seemed possibly useful as a basis for further questions and was thus repeated and approved, albeit rather hesitatingly. Before long, via pupils' talk of muscles and work, the teacher found himself back at his starting point of asking what food provided and receiving the answer *strength*. Asking then for another word for *strength*, he luckily found a pupil venturing the word *energy*. At this the teacher used all his reinforcements. He expressed approval of the pupil; he agreed with the answer; he repeated it; he awarded a team point; and he emphasised that *energy* was a good word. His approval seemed almost excessive, and he neither asked the pupil what was meant by the word nor explained why he thought it such a good one. Nevertheless he proceeded to try to elaborate the concept by talking of using petrol to keep a car going as analogous to eating food to keep a person working; and then he asked what the petrol changes to. Instead of the expected answer *energy* he got *smoke, water*, and *fire*, until some pupil ventured *energy*, presumably remembering it to be a good word! It is very doubtful whether any of the pupils in that lesson gained as much grasp of the concept as the teacher wished, for it is not possible to engage the thinking of a whole class in such an enterprise without giving more explicit direction and clearer definition of what is to be learned. What kind of word is *energy* besides being a good one? How does it relate to *work* and *movement*? How does it relate to *food, petrol,* and *electricity*? How does it relate to the common use of *energetic* and *being full of energy*? Perhaps some of these questions would not be thought appropriate for 10-year-olds, but if the concept is presented as it was in the above lesson some of the children might well be left in some mental confusion. They could be tending to explore some of the necessary thinking but be frustrated by lack of direction.

In another lesson the idea of latent heat was introduced to 12-year-olds. Some attempt was made to explain the concept, and a demonstration was given of the measurement of the temperature of water in a calorimeter before adding ice and after its melting. The necessary measures of weight were taken, and the class was presented with a computation. Afterwards one of the more intelligent pupils, with the experiment described in her notebook, was heard to complain that she didn't know what the experiment was meant to show and, more basically, that the difference between *heat* and *temperature* was not clear. In order for her to feel certain that she held something of the distinction, it was necessary to discuss the effects of supplying heat to saucepans of vegetables to boil water to cook them, of using a candle flame to melt ice in a frozen pipe, of feeling the heat from the sun warm the skin, and so on. Then, and only then, did the experiment make sense—that to measure temperature change was a way to calculate an amount of heat.

While the exchanges we have just discussed were from class teaching contexts, the following took place in another commonly found teaching situation when pupils are working in teacher-directed groups. In an environmental studies lesson the boys were exploring the reactions of various metals to atmospheric conditions, and the particular group quoted was engaged in the problem of rusting. Having found that tin cans rusted, they had concluded that tin rusted. The teacher was not certain why they were arranging their experiments on the assumption that their conclusion was correct, and the boys had no idea that they were wrong. The discussion was an attempt to clarify matters; and the extract gives the flavour of it and shows how an informal context lacks the formal modes of address, how the pupils talk more, and how the teacher's talking is less like a programmed text. It also shows the pupils asking spontaneous questions both for understanding and to make suggestions, as in *What do you mean?* and *How about chrome?*. The guidance to the pupils is relatively thin, however, and it may be no surprise to learn that when interviewed later they showed much confusion over the nature of tin and of tins as cans.

Teacher: No, look up tin I said, not metal; the word tin. Look up the word tin.
Boy: (several minutes later) Tin doesn't rust.

Teacher: All right—well if they are rusting then they are not tin, are they? So what else do you think they might be? (Several minutes elapse, during which time other children's problems are being discussed.)

Teacher: Now what I was trying to get at here is that if this was tin as you said it wouldn't rust, would it?

Boy: Well that isn't tin is it?

Teacher: It looks like tin.

Boy: Looks like it, yeh.

Teacher: I mean does a metal have to be one thing?

Boy: What do you mean?

Boy: It could be a mixture.

Teacher: Yes, do you know what we call a mixture of metals incidentally? ... Well never mind. You see you could have two metals there you know.

Boy: Aluminium.

Teacher: Well I mean, this is aluminium isn't it? Does it look like it?

Boy: Bit like this one.

Boy: How about chrome?

Teacher: Well chrome is something that they use to put on top of something else. You know you plate it; something could be chromium plated. Now I think you'll find ... and it would probably be easier if I tell you this. You'll find that this is actually made of steel underneath here. Now will steel rust?

Boy: Yes.

Teacher: Well obviously if you are going to have food and things in there you don't want it to rust, do you?

Boy: No.

Teacher: So what do you do then to stop it rusting?

Boy: Plate it with tin.

Teacher: That's right. This is actually what we would call tin plate.

The discussion of dialogues about energy and rusting have brought us to a consideration of the more specific problems of special subject teaching in secondary schools. These language problems are basically independent of such issues as the classifying of knowledge in the curriculum, for although concept attainment is context-sensitive as to particular aspects of selection and ways of presentation, it is independent in that it rests in human intelligence in a complex art of communication which encompasses all kinds of curricula. Thus the principles underlying our comments on learning within, say, physics will also be applicable in other traditional areas of learning, as well as in more newly defined areas such as integrated science. Broadly speaking, these principles are those of concept formation within adolescent intelligence, of selection of terminology according to value systems, and of the network of connections between specific terminology and the whole language of the subject area.

Barnes (1969) discussed some aspects of these issues in relation to lessons with 11-year-olds and made several points arising from his observations of the language used. Presentation of information and recall of 'facts' were very obvious, but explanation of processes and of the use of words was not, so that guided mental discovery was not well developed. Pupils' contributions from their own experience or from their questionings were slight, and seemed sometimes to be discouraged by the teacher's steamroller approach—a solid, straight-line attack along a predetermined path. Barnes also pointed out that it seemed highly likely that children were learning not only to restrict themselves to giving approved answers, but also to judge subjects differently according to the extent to which this kind of restriction was felt to operate. The sciences might seem to the children to be bodies of approved facts while English might seem a more open and intellectually and emotionally engaging subject. In other words, the style of classroom discourse could have important consequences for pupils' preferences for and views of subjects, and even for their wish to learn at all.

In chapter 2 we indicated some of the intellectual aspects of the attainment of concepts and the grasp of relationships involved in learning in adolescence, and we pointed to the way terms and expressions are learned not as separate 'bricks' of language but as parts of a network of a system in use. An interesting feature of the terminology of subject teaching to which Barnes drew attention is that a technical term often has a synonym in everyday use. While the teacher uses the synonym to help establish the meaning of the new technical term his own thinking is more geared to the network of meanings in the technical subject language than is that of the pupils. If the latter are thinking primarily in terms of everyday associations then mismatch which is not realised or resolved can occur between understandings. Barnes used the terms *trachea* and *wind-pipe* to make his point, but he also noted that the teacher who emphasises the former is not only introducing the term, but also indicating his own valuing of his subject as a specialism.

A further point made by Barnes was that each subject carries more than its specialist vocabulary, for this is set in the characteristic phraseology to such an extent that it is legitimate to speak of subject registers. But while teachers are often aware of introducing new terms, and pay attention to their definition, they are much less aware of the whole style of subject talk. This means that, unless the pupil can read sense into it, much of what the teacher says may not be comprehended and may therefore be learned by heart simply for reproduction, or dismissed. The accompanying feelings of insecurity and helplessness may positively turn the pupil away from attempting to learn, and may induce further feelings of dislike of the subject and antagonism towards those who can cope with it. Barnes indicated that where pupils contribute to the lessons their offerings are acceptable to the extent that they conform to the subject register, but that neither teacher nor pupil is aware that their speech indicates whether or not they belong to the same club. How pupils come to take up the register is a complex question. In part it may be the outcome of a gradual move into such speech throughout school life, but it may also be that children who have access to alternative sources of information such as specialist non-fiction, appropriate television and radio programmes, and subject-oriented conversations with persons outside school, are in a position to make better sense of the teacher's talking and to take part in discussion on his terms. And make sense of it they must, for the gist is not obvious. Any examination of teachers' talking shows much to be constructed of partially formed and poorly related remarks. Barnes (1969, p. 52) gave the following example:

'If we did it using a different method actually ... where we heat up the grass with acetone actually ... heating it under, er ... an enclosed system except ... I'll have to show using a diagram on that ... well er ... under reflux conditions so that we didn't lose the acetone then we could actually finish up with the grass a white colour.'

While Barnes was concerned principally with subject registers, Bellack and others (1966) attempted an analysis of teaching strategies as a context for their consideration of classroom language. These were, however, fairly general, recognising that activities tended to move in cycles of setting up a sequence, questioning the pupils and receiving their answers. Reactions by pupils or teachers involving explanation or evaluation of remarks were nested in these sequences. Sinclair and Coulthard (1975) developed this kind of analysis of the functions of speech in classroom exchange, but the use of language as part of the teaching-learning relationship was not pursued further. Walker and Adelman (1975), on the other hand, did define different overall teaching styles which related to the structure of verbal exchange. They discussed *focusing* as a strategy in which the teacher operates tight control to guide the pupils through specific questions and definitions to a predetermined end. They saw the *Cook's tour* as containing the same precision of question and answer, but as including a variety of end points; while *freewheeling* was seen as a strategy of allowing the pupils to make unpredictable contributions and encouraging open discussion of a more loosely defined theme. These styles can be seen to be related not only to teachers' personally preferred techniques but also to the nature of the intended learning.

These approaches remind us that teaching and learning are not simply conversations, but that effective instruction requires thoughtful planning and clear intent on the part of the teacher. This is as true of the 'open discussion' or 'creative writing' lesson as of that in which the transmission or evocation of more tightly specified knowledge is attempted. Smith and Meux (1970) discussed in detail the relationship between forms of speech and the logical content of a lesson. The total verbal behaviour in a lesson was referred to as the discourse, and this was analysed into tactics within overall strategies serving the purposes of the lesson. Discourse therefore served the teaching and learning; but it was not itself the lesson. The main functions of remarks were definition, explanation and evaluation, and a wide range of possible tactics lay within these categories. Additional utterances or aspects of utterances served management purposes. Within episodes teachers ideally needed to monitor pupils' responses to evaluate their logic, truth and correctness; but in practice they might often be handicapped by prior expectations, textbook requirements and the difficulty of relating the actual remarks to the thinking behind them.

Some examples of pupil and teacher failure to achieve logical clarity were given. If the teacher should ask *What does sentiment mean?* he may not be clear himself as to whether he will be satisfied with a definition or a description, and if he should ask *What is sentiment?* he may think he has asked for a definition but the form of the question may encourage the pupil to treat the abstract term as if it had concrete reference. The requirements for logical clarity are obviously demanding, but when they are not met (as will inevitably happen with the teacher thinking on his feet) there is ample room for confusion in the pupil's mind. The following episode is given as illustrating vague definition:

Pupil: What is a tariff wall?
Teacher: All right, both sides have tariffs. One side puts up a wall. Well ... well why does a nation have tariffs? Come on, answer your own question.
Pupil: Well, I don't understand what a wall is.
Teacher: I'm asking you a very simple question.

The pupil has not grasped the metaphoric use of the word *wall*, but the teacher seems oblivious of the nature of the problem, concentrating on the *tariff* half of the expression. This particular example also serves, however, to show how the language of control is intimately bound with that of the content of learning. It is interesting to see that, following the pupil's initiative, the teacher's response contains expressions that would not be permitted if the exchange were reversed. The relative status, threatened in the pupil's questioning, is preserved by use of the imperative *Come on, answer* ..., and by the implication of stupidity on the part of the student in ... *a very simple question*. Obviously, utterances can carry several kinds of meaning.

Before concluding our discussion of classroom language we should turn our attention for a while from the teacher-pupil exchange to the talking between pupils. This may take place within whole class activity, but often occurs when small groups are formed for some purpose. Britton (1969) and Barnes (1976) have attempted to explore children's talking in groups, both seeing it as a means of learning. Barnes wished to explore the pupils' potential contribution to classroom learning; but although he considered conditions that were likely to interfere with learning, he did not make clear how talking positively related to it. His sub-headings *Learning by talking* and *Learning in small groups* imply a necessary connection, but while Barnes admitted uncertainty about the necessity he did not take up the question of evaluating the learning. He turned instead to examining the actual language used by the children, inferring learning in some discussions but not in others. It is true the exchanges between pupils would fit his interpretations of the situations but the following considerations suggest they do not necessarily do so. The basis of his work was the observation of groups of 12- and 13-year-olds attempting to deal with set tasks in Science, English and History. In the Science task, which was to carry out some simple experiments on air pressure and to explain the findings, some groups employed probing questions and set up interesting suggestions; but this was by no means true of all; and rather than pointing to the value of talking as a means of learning the exercise seemed to indicate the pupils' varying needs for adequate guidance. Moreover, since the tasks were based on previous instruction, and the pupils were actually directed to explain in *the correct terms*, they were not tapping the children's learning through discussion so much as probing their ability to recall ideas already introduced. The distinction can be illustrated as follows. One group explained milk rising in a drinking straw in terms of suction. For them the answer to the set question *Why are you able to drink in this way?* was *It's the suction, I think*. The group agreed that this was an adequate answer. Another group pursued the explanation in terms of air pressure inside and outside the straw—an explanation according with the overall instruction to use the correct terms, which were those previously used by the teacher. Given the nature of the task, it would seem appropriate to evaluate the attempted explanations as efforts to recall a particular kind of account rather than as attempts to work out a satisfactory version in the pupils' own terms. Barnes in fact appeared to judge what was happening in terms of the former, but did not make it clear why he regarded the 'right kind' of explanation as also showing greater understanding, or why he thought that the suction explanation indicated an inadequate understanding of the physics rather than of the instructions.

Further points left unexplored were that drawing on existing talking competence is not necessarily a way of extending it (and there was no evidence given of pupil improvement in this respect), and that talking is not necessarily an index of thinking. The claim that *'Talking her way into a problem is enabling this girl to monitor her own throught and reshape it'* (Barnes, 1976, p. 28) is founded on an unproven supposition. We have already pointed out that talking may or may not indicate the fullness and the structure of a person's thinking. This being so, the observer cannot be sure that the children's talking indicated change in either the ability to discuss or the ability to think. Nevertheless, if Barnes was making a less strong claim about children's discussion—namely, that it can prove to be rich enough to be useful for the teacher in the guidance and development of further work—then the illustrations he gave would support it well. That the strength of his claim is not clear would seem to be due to an insufficient analysis of the nature of teaching and learning. On the one hand learning by discovery is valued, as is freedom in communication, and on the other hand verbal instruction of passive pupils is disapproved of; but the marriage of discovery with instruction, which is the essence of education, is not worked out with respect to goal agreement, ways of learning, the use of feedback and the nature of insight.

Britton, however, clearly asked the question as to whether in group discussion any real change takes place in the understanding of any of the pupils. While acknowledging that no necessary change follows and that evaluating is difficult, he claimed that his observations indicated likelihoods of change of several kinds. A pupil less adept than another at some skill seems likely to learn more through observation of its exercise; understanding seems likely to be enhanced if a speaker is required to explain his statements; and in problem solving two heads together might prove better than two apart. Britton's claim for advantage in pupils' exchanges with each other over teacher-pupil exchange alone tends to rest mainly in the greater freedom, greater mutual sympathy, and lesser inhibition in talking with each other. But to go beyond Britton's position, to try to evaluate the learning involved, some specification of what it might be and how far such change takes place is required. Guidance in such an enterprise can be obtained from such studies as those summarised in Sprott's (1958) review. A full analysis of children's talking in groups would require treatment of the formation of goals and norms of behaviour in the social interactions that develop. Chatter to friends often accompanies group and individual work—a social satisfaction which may enhance or detract from learning. Studies of small groups engaged in various tasks have shown a complex interaction between members—a setting in which a contribution is likely to depend on the person's actual resources for the task, his wish for approval or liking, and the extent to which his effort gives him power and arouses feelings of respect or liking or hostility in other members. Learning in groups is in principle no different from learning in teacher-pupil exchange, though in practice the flavour might be very different.

After reviewing the nature of classroom language we are able to see how complex a matter it is, how different the ideals and realities of the use of language in education can be, and how effective instruction depends on the teacher's mastery of a variety of its functions. As a final point we may ask how verbal behaviour in classrooms relates to the concepts of elaborated and restricted codes. We may recall that restricted codes are found amongst groups of persons, whatever their background, who share unexpressed assumptions and whose behaviour is strongly influenced by positional rather than interpersonal values. The elaborated code is available to those who are able to communicate effectively by making assumptions more explicit, and by using abstractions which carry more general or universal meanings than those pertaining to restricted groups. Since the forms of knowledge valued in traditional education tend towards abstract and universal symbolic systems, restricted code users have been said to be at a disadvantage. But our review in this chapter may well have set some readers wondering whether the term restricted does not well apply to particular classroom codes. Is the disadvantage, if any, due as much to a perpetuation by the school of restricted code use rather than to an inability on the part of children to enter into the elaborated code? Fishman (1965), discussing speech in multilingual societies, pointed out that switching from one dialect to another, and even from one language to another, was motivated in part by the interpersonal role and status relationships and in part by the topic of conversation. If the topic, or what is talked about in the classroom, indicates a selection of code (elaborated) that is at odds with that suggested by role and status considerations (restricted), then perhaps this is a major problem in education.

6

Literacy and Learning

Literacy is a large topic, and in this chapter we shall simply attempt to comment fairly generally on learning to read and write, on the relationship between literacy and speech, and on the ways in which the written word may be used in instruction and learning.

In previous chapters we have claimed that most young children have a useful command of their native tongue by the time they enter school and that their skill matures during the school years. Oral language problems in education tend to be associated with speech pathology or generally slow learning; or, more frequently, with marginally impoverished or inappropriate learning in terms of school experiences; or, most often, with failure to establish adequate and appropriate teacher-pupil communication in the classroom. But problems of written language skills are not similarly based. Learning to read and write begins later than learning to speak, and is not so fundamental to social interaction. People can do without the skills, though in a society in which all are expected to become literate to some extent doing without can be a severe trial in adult life and a cause for shame and anxiety during the school years. Furthermore, it can bar the way in further education, training and employment. It is, therefore, a matter of concern that many children appear to find reading difficult and do not acquire much skill. From the evidence collated in the Bullock Report (1975) it seems that approximately 20 per cent of 7-year-olds are virtually non-readers, while 4 per cent of 15-year-olds can only read as well as a 7-9-year old, and over 10 per cent read less well than the average 11-year-old. While the problems of testing and interpreting test results are difficult, it is nevertheless clear that in spite of being in school for some years many children profit little from reading instruction.

The efficacy of school instruction has been questioned from time to time when reading standards have been judged to have fallen, and writers such as Holt (1971) and Kohl (1975) have been very critical. Yet it is possible that out-of-school experience is also important both in success and failure. The early stages of literacy often precede schooling, and for older children reading in the everyday world outside may flourish relatively independently of school activities. This can be true both for children from very varied social backgrounds and also for children with quite marked differences in general intellectual ability and in oral verbal skill. It is important, therefore to consider learning to read and write both inside and outside school.

Although attempts to teach 2-year-old children to recognise printed words can be successful (Doman, 1964) the rate of learning is slow, and it is more commonly the case that no intentional instruction is attempted until much later. Meanwhile children learn to read signs and labels on buses, cans of food, packets and shops; and they also begin to grasp that long signs are read from left to right, and that newspapers and letters have to be held the right way up. Where they see others reading books, whether by themselves or in reading stories aloud, they begin to learn something of the correct orientation of reader to page. They are given toys, pictures and picutre-books to hold the right way up, and are shown how to work them and to turn the pages. All this—and yet no intentional teaching to read. For some children the introduction to literacy is more active. Torrey (1973) described how a child from a very impoverished home and with a non-standard dialect pressed his mother to inform him about words on food packages and the like, and how, out of the knowledge he obtained, he was able to begin to read new words. When I was talking with 5-year-olds about reading, one boy was able to tell me how to recalled beginning to read at about 3 years old and how he continued to learn. His grandmother looked after him when his sister was born, and after this initial help he felt he had learned mostly by himself. He was undoubtedly an extremely competent reader for his age. Clark (1975) reported some of the characteristics of children who began to learn to read before entering school and were quite able readers on entry. Her observation that the initial motivation often appeared to have come from the child is important in relation to our argument that effective instruction requires some learning contract. In many cases the children seemed to be taking the principal steps in forging some agreement about learning to read, for parents frequently felt some diffidence, doubt and even embarrassment about taking a teaching role. It is interesting that such a strong connection was present in parental minds between reading and teaching, whereas in other skill areas such as speaking and playing no such connection seemed to be made. It is often also observed in parents of less advanced readers, whose children have, nevertheless, shown an inclination to learn to read in out-of-school contexts, and it continues to be a source of anxiety to parents after their children have 'officially' begun to read in school.

Clark also observed that the parents of early able readers were, whatever their own education background, sensitive to the children's needs in terms of precision of guidance cues and appropriateness of information given. They also read to their children, and made use of whatever symbols in the environment attracted the children's attention. They tended to use libraries, and introduced their children to a variety of library books, catering for interests which showed not only individuality but also sex-role differentiation. One is reminded ot the careful and appropriate guidance given by some mothers in the problem-solving tasks in the Hess and Shipman study referred to in chapter 4. Nevertheless it is not the case that the children of parents with these qualities are always good readers. Some children do not play either wn initiating or a sustaining role in the learning interaction.

Clark commented on the perseverance shown by the able youngsters, and practice is an aspect of learning to read that cannot be overestimated. This does not necessarily imply reading and re-reading exactly the same items, though sometimes children enjoy doing so; but it does mean frequent attempts to try to read, so practising established skill in the context of seeking even more. In my own account of primary school children's reading experiences between 5 and 7 years (Francis, 1975) I found that while most children knew what it was for a parent to read to them, and most reported that they tried to read by themselves, only the better readers reported trying to read to a parent. Interestingly, this applied across a wide social class spectrum, and, while both fathers and mothers read to their children, mothers were by far the more frequent listeners to their children's attempts. Thus the better readers were not only having more success with their silent reading but were also gaining information about the correctness of their interpretations. There was some suggestion in my study that parents had implicit views about the nature of reading skill, for the practice of reading aloud to children dropped away dramatically as the children themselves became able to read stories, or as they began to be defined at school as good or poor readers. It was as if parents said that the children were becoming too old, and for the good readers a good job had been done but for the poor readers little more could be expected. Furthermore, the patterns of provision of books in the home seemed to suggest that some parents viewed ability to read a simple book or a comic as enough preparation for whatever reading was required in life, while others had notions of progress through books of increasing variety and difficulty within the range of children's literature, leading on to a move into adult literacy. But a poorly provided home did not always indicate a limited view. Access to libraries could make a world of difference. Bullock (1975) indicated that children's libraries and mobile library facilities can be and have been used to good effect.

Literacy demands that we have both authors and readers, and schooling demands that each pupil both reads and writes. Although reading is given some primacy in schools, each child is expected to express much of his learning in writing and so inform his teachers of his successes and failures in a variety of topics. Often children are encouraged to write in the early stages of reading, and word building with plastic letters, as well as attempted writing, can be used to help them learn the forms of words they choose to know as well as those they are given to learn. Methods of instruction vary both in the stress laid on various reading sub-skills at different stages and in the extent to which individual instruction is practised. It is beyond the scope of this book to discuss them, but all have in common some of the characteristic features of instruction—the learner may or may not be actively and willingly involved, he may not grasp the point of what he is being asked to do, and the learning may seem far removed from the world outside. It is doubtful, though, whether the child entering school is disinclined to learn to read, even if he does not know what it is about; but many are neutral and feelings of failure in the early stages can engender a definite dislike. In my own study of fifty children observed for two years, several grew unhappier as they approached 7 and it became clear to them that they could not read as well as other children. In fact they could scarcely recognise more than a few words and had difficulty in trying to make sense of new words, either in isolation or in context. This was after two years of schooling, during which time those children who had entered reading well had further increased their skill while many others were making such progress that both they and their teachers were happy enough.

Wherein lies the difficulty then? We must look beyond the question of mental ability for although low intelligence may be associated with slow learning some severely subnormal children do manage to achieve some reading skill, while some children of high ability experience much more than average difficulty in learning to read. We must also go beyond questions of special disabilities related to reading—difficulties of a perceptual or dyslexic nature—for many slow or non-readers have no such diagnosed handicaps.

What is sometimes proposed as an answer to the question is found in the Bullock Report's introduction which sees literacy as being intimately associated with oral language skill. It has been commonly supposed that learning to read depends on some level of spoken language acquisition, but such is the complexity of both skills that such a statement is often doing no more than relating the unspecified to the unspecifiable. It involves such difficulties as the following. When does pre-reading become reading? Are reading sub-skills acquired in a specifiable order? How does one determine a level of language acquisition? Without some clear definition of what is being talked about it is impossible to try to establish that any particular kind of learning must necessarily precede another. And even if some broad correlation is found between speech skills and literacy it is still possible that they are relatively independent and each rests on some other common factor.

Such research findings as we have suggest that we would be unwise to assume a necessary relationship between speech structure (excluding those children with speech pathologies) and initial learning to read. Some children learn to read simple sentences and stories while their speech is still characteristic of 3-4-year-olds. Soderbergh (1971) made a special detailed study of such learning. Many others begin to read labels and occasional words and phrases at the same stage. Torrey (1973) told of a pre-school child from a very disadvantaged home. In my own work (Francis, 1974b) I found no correlation between the syntactic structure of children's speech in situations which seemed to maximise their performance and their word recognition and early sentence reading abilities up to the age of 7. Similar findings were reported by Strickland (1962) and Loban (1963). Early reading seems to make more demand on attention, recognition and association skills than on knowledge of language. Studies such as Torrey's suggest that the differences in form between non-standard dialect and the language of textbooks need make little difference to early learning of reading. Many of our primary school children begin to read in spite of pronounced regional dialects, and some do so very well indeed.

There may, however, be other relationships between oral language and early reading that bear further investigation. My own work showed a correlation of initial reading skill with vocabulary test scores; and there was a further correlation with amount of speech in a tester-testee story-telling context, but only for children of more disadvantaged backgrounds. The nature of the words sampled in the vocabulary and word recognition tests suggested either that a better vocabulary aided reading—possibly facilitating word recognition—or that some common drive or ability to learn underlay both. That those relatively disadvantaged children who talked more to a 'middle-class' tester were better readers than their class-mates, suggested that maybe they were able to learn more effectively within school by engaging in more verbal exchange with teachers or, again, that their fluency and reading ability rested on some other common factor. Slow learning may therefore be due not so much to any overall language disability as to specific kinds of disadvantage related to the uses to which speech may be put by young children.

One of these uses is to talk about spoken language in such a way that children can relate such talking to description and analysis of the written version. If a child has not realised that he can, so to speak, take the spoken word out of the everyday stream of events in which it is used and mentally turn it over or actively talk about it with someone else, then he has not attained an abstractive skill which Vygotsky (1962) has stressed. This reflection on the use of the spoken word, implying such questions as *What did he say?* and *What did he mean?* is possibly a very valuable aid to asking the same questions of isolated written words, sentences and continuous prose.

Further uses of speech in learning to read are talking about the nature and purposes of reading, and explanation of the technical vocabulary of instruction and of learning the forms of language. Reid (1966) explored children's ideas about reading, and found that 5-year-olds had very uncertain notions about its nature. They also confused the meanings of terms like *word, sentence, letter* and *number* and of *reading* and *sounding*. Downing (1970) found similar confusion. In my own study (1973) it was evident that technical terms became clearer to the children between 5 and 7 years but that the children were seeking their meaning through their use in relation to reading materials. Whether more explicit reference to their meaning by the teachers would have facilitated learning their use was an open question, but it was shown that the children's general vocabulary command was such as to challenge any suggestion that the terms were too abstract for the children. Perhaps some children learn slowly simply because they are not clearly guided, no matter what method of instruction is adopted.

In large classes one might suppose that some children will not be sufficiently helped, but matters are not as clear-cut as that. Various studies, including Morris's (1966) survey, have shown that size of class has little effect on reading ability, and the Bullock Report suggests that the larger classes may indeed yield better reading standards. It is clear that individualised instruction, which may be facilitated by smaller classes, is likely to benefit the pupil maximally, but there is also the possibility that such instruction may not be effectively carried out, and some children may even set themselves a slow pace. In large classes teachers are more aware of their teaching burden and may teach more effectively, either by deliberately making better individual or small group provision or by requiring that all pupils attend to some planned series of lessons and exercises in systematic class instruction. Here we suggest that, other things being equal, teaching style may be more important than methods of instruction, and certainly this was the main message of the Morris study. It is reinforced by Southgate's work (Southgate, 1966), in which the importance of a 'reading drive' in school is noted. This may well parallel the 'reading drive' seen in those homes where children's reading is encouraged and supported. But what of the children themselves? We have already pointed to differences between children in interest, drive and perseverance, and to the cumulative effects of these on reading skill. Success goes to the successful, while difficulty and lack of learning breed dissatisfaction, hostility and a sense of failure. One of the toughest assignments for the primary school teacher is to support, guide and sometimes even to drive the slow learners to levels of skill in which they can feel some personal satisfaction and some social approval.

In doing this they may well ask to what ends children should be encouraged to learn to read. First we should perhaps be clear that it is not to satisfy some general demand about maintaining reading standards or reaching some specified level appropriate to age. These are measures of certain kinds of achievement, not aims of education. Secondly we must recognise that aims will be varied and not always suited to all children. In general, however, we should surely hope to see to it that our children leave school able to read and write sufficiently well to manage the signs, the instructions, the newspapers, and the form filling and letter writing necessary for comfort, safety, friendship and family interests and satisfactory job performance. This I shall call basic social writing competence, and it may have little to do with reading books. A further aim, in a society where literature is an art form, must be to make it possible for children and adults to read and write prose and poetry, for pleasure in the content and delight in the form. Additionally it should be made possible for those whose interests and abilities take them that way to be able to read and write what is needed to enable them, and to qualify them, to carry on any kind of work that requires reference to the written records of events or work in past times or in other places, whether written by themselves or by others.

Such persons will include teachers, but it is not the case that what literacy has meant to them is neccessarily what it must mean to all whom they teach. The teacher does not automatically and necessarily simply pass on his own experience. He is an agent in a much wider picture of transmission.

How do children fare at gaining social reading competence in schools? A general impression is that teachers see such competence as an incidental rather than a central concern—that pre-reading skills are expected to be rooted in the beginnings of such a competence, but that they predominant aim is to teach the children to read and write within the terms of a school curriculum that is rather separated from the rest of life. At the secondary school level, however, for those children who are such slow learners and perhaps also poor readers that they are virtually 'rejects' of the school system, attention may be focused on reading and writing for social competence as a step towards the transition from school to work. Thus, instead of being seen as an essential part of normal education it tends to be regarded as something for babes or fools—or, in reaction against just consideration of its place, as something which only those superminds who can decipher and understand social security and tax forms and rulings can be expected to achieve. But the truth of the matter is that many families are deprived of benefits to which they are entitled and services to which they could have access because fathers and mothers are frightened of the written word or do not feel competent to use it. Instructions at work—on bottles, packets and clothing, and those to do with travelling—are mis-read; consequently delay, discomfort and accident are needlessly suffered. Much of the competence needed is to be found in the ability to understand isolated words functioning as signs, phrases and headlines which convey meaning without being fully grammatical, and sentences with one or two clauses of up to eight words or so—with the proviso that they contain the appropriate vocabulary. The ability to write personal and family details, to write requests and instructions relating to earning and spending, and to apply for jobs, requires similar written linguistic skill. These skills are related to the abilities of the 10-year-old reader, but in school such skill is usually directed towards simple prose and poetry and books containing information of use for projects and similar school exercises. Yet, if social reading competence is neglected in favour of more valued educational aims, the less able readers and the poorer spellers can lose confidence in their ability to manage their basic social needs in this respect, and they can learn to dodge rather than to use the written word. Alienation from basic literacy may not be due so much to the artificiality of content and form of many school readers as to the failure to link any kind of reader or story-book to fundamental real-life use of reading and writing.

The second aim mentioned above—to encourage and appreciate reading and writing of prose and poetry—is a dominant theme in schools, with the emphasis on reading selections of published works approved by the teacher and on writing according to the child's personal expression. This is evident in the Bullock Report, which only pays lip-service to our first aim. The principal reason would seem to be a definition of mature reading—the goal of school instruction—as the ability to read continuous prose with speed and understanding. It is undoubtedly true that such reading is more readily achieved with age, but it is too easy to slip from this into thinking that it is the most important reading skill for mature persons. We have, however, made our present priorities clear, and can take a closer look at our second aim.

Once launched from a reading scheme, or having somehow attained the ability to attempt simple continuous prose, the primary school child is encouraged to read fiction. Connie and Harold Rosen (1973) claim that 'For young children the real book is a storybook,' and emphasise the possibilities of intimate involvement in the reading matter. Fiction is seen as a way of symbolising the world of feeling, and a child's being drawn to a particular book as a complex educational affair. Fiction is also seen as an extension of meeting and conversing with other people—an extension of the experience of oral language. We are reminded, when we think of Jones's (1968) criticisms of use of project materials, that the same points might also be made about non-fiction. And often books purporting to be informative, as in the case of travel books, history and biography, are written in a fictional style for young children. We may wonder about the problems of separating fact from fiction and of accuracy in information, but often when we do we forget the fickleness of memory and the need for repetition within a framework of knowledge built up over literally years of experience before truth, falsehood and accuracy become pressing concerns. We forget what it is to be a child.

It is easy, too, to forget that many children read slowly; that a whole page is an effort; that what is coming in the text is not very obvious, so that it is harder to understand the immediate words (Neville and Pugh, 1974). A sense of intimacy or excitement may make all the difference between continuing or ceasing to read, and all the difference between taking up another book or turning away from such reading. And alas for the person who is very particular about the choice of reading material, for it may not be the written word that immediately attracts or the beauty of the ideas behind it, but rather some feature of the illustrations or the excitement of a chase in a fairly crude account. Every teacher and every parent who has views about the relative desirability of various kinds of literature for children will know the feeling of wishing to discourage some without at the same time reducing the child's interest in reading.

Reading interests have been described by Whitehead and others (1975) and by Hayes (1975) in a useful review. It is apparent that some children are avid readers in spite of the attraction of alternative ways of spending their time, but that what they read is very varied in nature. The same child who at 14 reads Charles Dickens and Jane Austen with enjoyment will also read simple adventure stories with a narrative line full of action and thrills, a magazine or two relating to special hobbies or sex-role interests, comics and newspapers. In adolescence moods change markedly and, while reflective thought and artistic appreciation sometimes engage the attention, at other times the satisfaction of identifying with a hero or heroine in simple wish fulfilment gives ease to the developing identity, and at others the substitute excitement of aggressive and sexual interests is actively sought in reading.

But what of the less avid reader? Several studies find that the majority of children spend little time reading, and Hayes refers to a reading 'drop-out' of some magnitude—60 per cent of young people. Children who have learned to read continuous prose do not further develop this skill, but as adolescence advances read less, and often are interested almost entirely at the level we have called social reading competence. They sample, though to a lesser extent, the detective, horror, ghost and battle stories and the romantic and sex novelettes; they look at the cheaper newspapers and they read the odd book or magazine pertaining to a hobby or special interest. Other children, who have not even managed to read the simpler stories designed for 7-9-year-olds, can do no more than struggle with fragments of any reading that might interest them. Implicit in surveys of reading interests is the judgement that reading is good but that reading classical or 'quality' literature is better; and very evident is the finding that few children read very much, and that even fewer can enjoy, what was, after all, written for adults. While syllabuses for literature examinations require some adolescents to read classical literature, many teachers do draw upon a wider range of materials both for reading and for stimulating children's own writing. But the fact is that by adolescence many children find continuous prose beyond them, and that school experience has done little if anything, to fill the gap between very early learning to read and adult reading of cheaper newspapers, comics, and simple magazines.

How do homes and schools influence these patterns of reading interest and practice? We have seen that in early reading the more competent children experience a drive to read both at home and at school. The home experience may precede and certainly supplement the school experience. It may even be the framework for school learning. We have seen, too, that the child's own interest is crucial to his taking up that of his parents and teachers. At later stages a similar pattern is evident, but an additional factor emerges. Not only is adult interest important, but knowledge and provision of reading materials becomes a significant differentiator for children. I was impressed in my own survey of reading interests of two groups of 5-7-year-olds by the difference between those children who could anticipate reading fiction, non-fiction and poetry suitable for the 7-11 range and those who made no reference to anything but their own school readers and comics and the ghost, love and crime stories, the comics and the newspapers they claimed their parents enjoyed reading. The former group of children were predominantly middle-class, and were referring to books possessed by older siblings or being provided by parents and other relatives. They referred, too, to spending pocket-money on books, and, although they felt some freedom to choose when in a shop, they were obviously guided both to the shop and to suitable purchases by adults who wanted them to read. Yet not all the children of middle-class parentage reported such interest and practice, and not all those whose parents encouraged them expressed any real enthusiasm. While the purchase of books showed a middle-class bias, obtaining books from a library was mentioned more widely by both middle-class and lower working-class children, but the latter again seemed to lack knowledge of what might be available for them.

There is a case, then, for teachers and libraries to act in an advisory capacity. But Pugh (1971) found that while librarians' suggestions were in fact taken up by children, teachers did not always recommend books, and when they did their suggestions were not so readily adopted, either by the avid or the less avid readers. Morris's (1966) study also suggested that primary school provision of reading materials varied considerably, and the Bullock Report is very critical of provision in the secondary schools. One has the impression that children's reading in adolescence is scarcely, if at all, influenced by school experience. This impression is strengthened when one looks at the time given in school for 'private reading'. The proportion declines from the primary to the secondary stage, and different stress is laid upon its importance. Whereas in the first year or two of schooling reading is essential and is often promised as interesting and fun, in the later stages it becomes peripheral to school 'subjects' and is concentrated in literature lessons, or even allowed as a reward rather than as 'real work'. Hayes points out that children can come to regard private reading and school reading as quite separate, but perhaps it is more the case that, as with the more basic reading competence needed to get by in society, reading for pleasure and appreciation develops as an activity in which the school intervenes rather than as one which is essentially its province. Literature as an art form, as man talking to man about his ideas, his aspirations and his very nature, has after all more to do with life outside than inside the classroom. Furthermore, reading is an intimate rather than a public activity; the public aspect of literature is the author's writing. And this, surely, is the true focus of attention for the classroom as a place where appreciation, understanding and judgement can be enhanced by public discussion.

A third objective in teaching children to read is to extend learning in 'subject' knowledge and encourage demonstration of understanding through writing. We saw in chapter 5 how classroom talking provided both a way of subject learning and a social context in which it was attempted. The same may be said of reading and writing, although most discussion on literacy in schools fails to consider the learning context.

In primary schools, as the Bullock Report pointed out, children are not taught subject specialisms by specialist teachers, but encounter variously integrated curricula. But often there is a fairly clear distinction in teachers' and pupils' minds between reading and writing connected with prose and poetry and that connected with number work. Perhaps it is not always sufficiently appreciated how mathematics in school requires reading skills of the same order, and often exactly the same kind, as other work. The transition from using terms and sentence structures embedded in everyday speech to using mathematical symbols and statements is not clearly understood, but without the ability to read and write in either form the pupil is severely handicapped. As the secondary stage looms ahead, and especially in middle schools, more discrimination of subject areas is shown, and subject textbooks may be used. Often, however, it is assumed that pupils should be able to read them, and the problem of those who cannot, it is felt, is a problem for the specialist reading teacher. But, while it is true that certain pupils have particular reading difficulties, most of the problems of reading school textbooks rest within the relevant subject learning. In every kind of lesson older children not only need to be in command of a generally appropriate level of reading ability but, as in the case of oral language, need to be using their abilities to master the language of the subject. Learning a subject is learning its language—whether it be a traditionally bounded school subject or a part of one of the new curricula. And just as learning requires the construction of knowledge in the processes of talking, so it does in gaining meaning from a text.

Reading and writing in primary and middle schools, is not, however, irrelevant to that in the secondary. The attempt to forge understanding through talking finds its parallel in the reading and writing of school-children, and begins as soon as the child attempts some kind of continuous prose. Unfortunately, attitudes and abilities in writing may be affected by constraints which are not easily perceived by the teacher. Behind the more obvious effects of different handwriting, spelling and linguistic skills lie other features of writing in schools which may alter a child's interest and ability. One example is the effect of a writing 'overload'. In primary schools where a great enthusiasm for literacy is manifested, children are sometimes asked to write very frequently about their experiences, and sometimes children can be heard to anticipate with groans such words as, 'Now, children, I want you to write about ...'. Or, worse they come to avoid those activities which their teachers tend to select for writing. Thus I once observed a few 7-year-old boys choosing to stay at school to read rather than go for a walk in the nearby woods. They reckoned that the walkers would have something to write about, but that their teacher did not ask them to write after reading; therefore, although reading was difficult it was chosen because it was less painful than writing! A further factor, more common with older children, is that of using writing as a punishment. This is presumably done because some children already find it aversive, but such action is scarcely calculated to improve attitudes to writing, whatever the ability of the child. These illustrations serve to remind us that literacy within the curriculum, as with all forms of learning, requires a common teacher-pupil understanding of its place and agreements about its use. Unfortunately studies of middle and upper school reading and writing suggest more confusion than consensus.

In addition to reading and writing within the areas of literature and expressive writing, middle school children are often required to employ their skill in project work related to historical, scientific and social studies. Typical projects might be *Norman castles, Dinosaurs, Horses, Life in Ponds, Growing Cotton.* Sometimes they are related closely to lessons and available books in school; but sometimes they are unrelated, perhaps chosen by the child; and they require reference beyond the resources of the school. In either case they require similar searching and understanding, but in the former the teacher can more readily give guidance. Merritt (1971), Moyle (1975) and the Bullock Report all treat the question of the kind of guidance indicated. Outstanding features are help in finding data, help in deciding how to read for the purpose in mind, guidance in thinking while reading, and help in evaluating material for use. Finding data requires familiarity with catalogue systems and use of an index and of a contents list. It means acquiring a knowledge of what is likely to be found in advertisements, brochures, newspapers, magazines and reports, as well as what can be sought from books. It requires, too, the ability to relate pictures and diagrams to texts and, in contrast to reading a whole story, the ability to select from a book. Guidance in thinking about what is read means helping a pupil to find something he can personally understand, and helping him to master something of texts that are difficult for him. Evaluating what is read means guidance in judging how much confidence can be placed in accounts, by comparing them with the pupil's existing knowledge and with each other; it also means guidance in relating their contents to the use the pupil wishes to make of them. If the pupil is successfully helped in this way he is likely to find the use of textbooks in the secondary school an aid to learning, but if not he may be confirmed in a growing suspicion that books are not for him.

It is a matter for concern then, that teachers are not well prepared to aid pupils in this way, thinking that if they can read prose at all, and if a variety of books are made available, all will be well. But because teachers are ill prepared, and because resources are not all they might be in many a classroom, the schools often unwittingly sell children short. And if that is so, then differences in home provision may make considerable differences to later school performance. Now middle school children at home are, as we have already seen, differently provided with reading matter and reference resources—though use of libraries may mitigate the effects. But they are also differently provided with people who will help them with reading research skills. Middle-class children are likely to be better provided for, since it is more likely that their parents were relatively successful in their own secondary schooling. They will have more of an inkling of what is required, and they may be more willing to allow 'school' to invade 'home' and vice versa. But even within the middle-class sector there are considerable differences between families in this respect, and within families provision is not a one-way process. Only where the child concerned is willing to press forward with the project rather than simply to copy from his data will reading skill be effectively enhanced. What was true for early readers tends also to be true of successful readers later in school; and what is clearly evident is that subject forms of written language rest in a more general context of social exchange through reading and writing—exchanges between the learner, his friends, his family, his teachers, and all who have written whatever he reads, or read whatever he writes. And ultimately both rest in talking about aspects of literacy. When home and classroom conditions allow a fair exchange between learner and mentor and when literacy is valued, then a child's reading skills may develop beyond the levels of social adequacy and simple prose reading to take him into the community of those whose knowledge and life is immeasurably enriched by the communication across space and time of man's insights and understanding.

At the secondary school stage the importance of these skills becomes evident, and in each subject area they require fostering. A study by Gillard (1975), however, suggests that such care is not often exercised. He found that, while pupils' general prose reading skill correlated with their verbal reasoning scores, their skill at reading physics, chemistry and biology texts was much less well developed. And this was not merely a matter of unknown vocabulary, but also of the whole subject language register. It was concluded that the texts and pupils were in part ill matched, but also that the children were not being appropriately guided into use of the books. Here we have a direct comparison with Barnes's (1969) discussion of subject register in classroom talking. Rosen (1972) has explained the differences between register as found in texts and in pupils' writing. The register of a textbook is usually formal, the area of discourse being subject defined, often at a more abstract level than the pupil finds in speech and in fiction. There is a real danger that some pupils will be thought to be not intelligent enough to make sense of it, whereas they could more easily do so if guided into this adult and special way of writing. Without appropriate help from teachers some pupils will still be fortunate and determined enough to forge their way ahead; but others take refuge behind the routine repetition of forms of language they somehow know to be appropriate but fail to comprehend; and others still will come to regard textbooks and the language of subject specialisms as alien and beyond them. Rosen argues that children's writing can be guided towards appropriate expression by sensitive subject-teachers, and that there is a strong case for assessment and selection of textbooks, as well as intelligent use of them by both teachers and pupils. Gillard (1975) explored the factors behind the choice of textbooks and found that cost, syllabus coverage and academic level tended to determine selection, and that the pupils' reading skills were rarely taken into account. Moreover, the teachers were not at all well informed about reading skill and ways of exploring it.

When we look at the classroom context in which subject reading and writing take place, some observations of experience in secondary schools are disturbing. First, the actual provision of books is sparse. Often pupils are issued with books only during the relevant lesson, and in some cases they are not allowed to take them elsewhere in school or to take them home to work from them. Once a text is chosen and bought it may be some time before an addition or a substitution can be made. This relative lack of resources forces the classroom activity more towards teacher talk than towards a wider sampling of knowledge. Second, even where books are available, they are not used as much as they might be under teacher guidance. The pupil is left to work from them with very minimal help, and often with some confusion as to the nature of his search. Only too frequently children hear words such as 'Read pages 10-12 and be ready for a test'; and less often 'Read pages 10-12 and be ready to talk about them next lesson'. In these cases children tend to read the pages line by line—sometimes very painstakingly—but without selecting points of interest, defining sequences or explanations, or summarising and evaluating the content. Consequently they do not grasp ideas and their relations clearly, nor do they even build a framework to contain the relevant major facts bearing on the theme. When tested they remember virtually nothing, or produce parrot-like answers. Except for those who really were able to perform the intended task on their own, they might as well not have tried the reading. This situation parallels that of classroom talking. Only general instructions can be given to initiate activities, and competition between individuals for help with their work both leads to and is foiled by signs of boredom and frustration expressed in unrest. But although reading and writing can be so difficult, a very odd state of affairs can sometimes be observed: the pupils turn quietly to writing, as though thankful for a relatively peaceful classroom situation, though in fact they have very little of worth to write. They seem sometimes to conspire to force the teacher into presenting them with work-cards which give them a limited and defined task, or to evade thinking and exploring by reducing their writing virtually to copying or to reproducing the teacher's talking. Here one sees another example of a token acceptance of some aspect of literacy with a view to avoiding a proper effort and involvement. It is possible to see in the pupils' classroom behaviour the same group pressures and 'power politics' that we discussed in relation to learning through spoken language.

In chapter 4 we raised the question of whether pupils might be regarded as one or more cultures. While, since Deutsch and Bernstein raised the question it has been seriously discussed in relation to spoken language, it has for long been a debated question with respect to literacy. It might help to clarify matters if certain distinctions are examined. First, it is clear to us already that literacy may be regarded at several levels. There is illiteracy, literacy for day-to-day social competence and simple pleasure, and literacy which means involvement in transcultural exchange across time and space. The boundaries are not clear but the general orientation at each level is evident. The distinctions being made are not the consequences of universal formal education but lie in the general educative practices of the population concerned. Universal schooling might aim to enhance or to obliterate such distinctions as descriptive of adult literacy—and whatever its aims, it might nevertheless achieve one or the other. Second, the distinctions do not correlate at all well with occupation *per se*, for it is possible to find the different levels in all social ranks. Nevertheless, it is true that resources for literacy are more evident in homes with a sufficient margin of income—provided, that is, that the margin is spent in that way. This means that ultimately levels of literacy rest on value systems. Where reading is not seen as important, why learn?

Loughton (1969) described how a boy, whose ambition was to be a lorry driver, avoided the necessity of acquiring a basic social competence by depending on others. He was not even concerned about reading signposts since he reckoned he could always ask for advice—and many signs were wrong anyway! His father was scarcely literate in any sense of the word, and his mother could not read at all. They were unconcerned about both their own and their children's lack of competence. While similar families can no doubt be found, many of the adult illiterates see the point of social reading competence, even though they find it hard to overcome the shame and secrecy they feel about their own inadequacy. But where life is a daily struggle to provide for a family on very low wages or social security payments, where the material conditions of living require an almost endless round of hard labour with inadequate resources and with poor health, and where both minds and wills are dulled, reading competence seems almost a complete irrelevance. But it was the wish to teach children from homes like these that lay behind the provision of universal compulsory education—and not only to provide a better-equipped labour force for industry, but also to ensure that the children had a better chance than their parents of establishing homes fit for families. Although social conditions have greatly improved in the last century, there are still children from families where reading has no meaning and to them we owe the fostering of a basic competence as an educational priority. While agreeing with Postman (1970) that to teach reading is to take a political position on how people should behave and on what they ought to value, I cannot entirely accept that it also necessarily induces conformity. The ability to read may give an individual the ability to follow instructions, but it does not lead him to follow them blindly. Conformity is a matter of personality and attitude that may well be affected by education—but it is a separate matter from the ability to read.

But it is not at the basic level of social and cultural deprivation that the debate about different cultures rages most. It is at the level of value systems that recognise the need for basic competence but query the point of any other reading. We have pointed to the error of equating these with social class, but there is a strong tendency for some writers to speak of different working-class and middle-class values in relation to literacy. This is particularly so with respect to curriculum decisions about what to teach to whom, and for our final consideration in this chapter we shall try to disentangle some of the features of literacy that add to the emergence of subcultures in secondary schools and the sort of conflict and disharmony that hinders rather than promotes learning. To do this we shall need to consider some of the aims of education, teachers' views and practices in relation to reading, and pupils' values as the outcome of their experience both at home and in school.

Lawton (1975) points to the fact that several educational thinkers who explore different aims nevertheless agree in seeing education as the transmission of culture. Hirst (1974), however, in seeing knowledge as trans-cultural, avoids devising curricula suited to different cultures. Presumably, with due respect to individual differences, all children should have access to a common body of knowledge and skill. Insofar as reading is both a skill and a means of constructing and sharing knowledge, it is for all pupils—whatever differences lie in the values of the social groups to which they belong, for these groups are in fact equally enmeshed in the common social structure. Bantock (1971) on the other hand, quoting Bernstein and Jensen in support of his argument, suggests an alternative curriculum for working-class children—one which is aimed at practical common concerns, which reduces dealing with the abstract, and which cultivates the emotions and activities for leisure. Such a curriculum would be liberal but would avoid the usual *concentration on reading* characteristic of *academic education* (my interpretation and my italics). Yet however one looks at the suggestion it contains nothing that could not be advocated for the middle-class child; but it minimises some very important aspects of education, and the grounds for this reduction are very dubious. Even if Bernstein is right in pointing to social class differences in language use, and even if Jensen is right in pointing to different kinds of intelligence (associative and conceptual), one might ask why education should contain these differences rather than transcend them. Further, one might ask why reading should be so heavily implicated, and why the middle-class alternative should be termed *academic*. A consideration of these questions leads one to think that Bantock has not clearly distinguished between what the pupil brings to his learning in terms of personality, ability and interest and what he needs in terms of a curriculum; nor has he distinguished curricula from ways of teaching. Certainly a curriculum can contain teaching which misuses reading and which fails to bring out the richness of the so-called academic for the individual, but this impinges on both middle- and working-class children, and to advocate less reading and thinking is not to advocate a different curriculum but only a poorer one.

This, of course, is a value judgement, and it is based not only on the assessment that something is missing in Bantock's non-academic curriculum, but also on the view that what is missing is worth having. Here one would criticise use of the word *academic* in that it can carry connotations of ivory towers, separation from reality, aridity and narrowness of thought, and so on. But a strong case can be made for treating literacy and recourse to books as essential features of modern culture. They illumine the play of man's transactions in society and tap the resources of the recorded observations, insights and judgements both of the forebears who set the stage for our present ways of living and of our contemporaries. 'Subject' study provides no more than exemplars of such tapping. If particular examples are found uninteresting this is no argument for abandoning the whole endeavour, or for leaving it only to a few with 'academic' orientations. Modern man, whatever his inclinations and whatever additional media of exchange are available, is ill equipped to understand what is happening to him, and what he might himself do, if he is unable to use the written word. His attention is restricted to the ongoing stream of events, and, being in a poor position to reflect on them himself, he is more vulnerable to propaganda, prejudice and ill-informed indoctrination. In spite of these comments, however, Bantock's considerations are important, for many sympathise with them; they have pointed to differences between pupils which are likely to affect their response to being expected or encouraged to read both in subject areas and in literature; and he has indicated that the values expressed in ways of teaching may well run counter to the pupils' own.

Since we have already indicated the nature of differences between pupils in relation to reading skills in secondary schools, we need only point out here that in paralleling difficulties with spoken language in classrooms they add to the pressures which result in the development of pro- and anti-school feelings, and thus give the impression of two 'literacy cultures'. Postman (1970) is right to point out how teachers tend to equate literacy with intelligence and to question this relation, but one can see how in schools the relationship of literacy with attainment easily leads to this assumption. It takes some perceptiveness to see that some of the adolescents who reject books in school were once 9-year-olds who read with interest, and that their present state is not entirely due to some inadequacy in them. One possible feature in the picture of their development is the effect on them of teachers' views on reading.

One obvious effect is that of the teachers' view that reading is more necessary and useful for those who aspire to further training and higher education. Not all teachers hold this view, but many nevertheless work in schools where it represents the prevailing ethos. Paralleling Bantock's considerations are teachers' decisions to use visual aids, concrete experience and talking more evidently with pupils of non-examination forms or groups. Pupils can therefore obtain less practice and guidance with reading, and can view reading interest and ability as a mark of the 'pro-school' culture. Another effect is that of subtly conveying that reading in subject areas is a chore rather than a pleasure. If studies of the reading abilities, interests and practices of students in higher education can be taken as any guide, then some teachers themselves may well carry something of this attitude with them. Ways of referring to the use of books can affect the pupils' attitudes; and in this respect even the 'examination pupils', whose reading abilities are good, may come to under-employ their skill (and neither they nor the teachers are helped when the textbooks are badly presented). A further feature of teachers' attitudes is found when texts are abandoned because they seem too difficult—because the pupils have to struggle with them. Perhaps sometimes it is forgotten that reading *is work*, and that it may be light or heavy without being inappropriate. In discussing the Humanities Curriculum Project, Stenhouse (1975) reported how the teachers assessed the level of reading materials as being more ambitious than any they had met before and how they found using them a struggle. Yet the pupils did show some improvement in reading comprehension, in vocabulary and in self-esteem as a consequence of working with the project. If teachers view reading as something which should readily yield immediate comprehension—a view that is easily held if most reading tests and light literature are the yardsticks—then much of the point of reading in learning may be missed. Then pupils who find reading and learning less easy than others may tend to identify reading with the more able groups and to regard it as not worth their while. Again such a tendency will reinforce the appearance of different subcultures.

From our previous considerations in this chapter we know which pupils are likely to be those in the 'low-reading culture'. They are those who, relative to their peers, began to fall behind in reading during their primary and middle school years, those who fall behind in general in their schoolwork, those who in spite of their abilities can see little point or value in school learning and reading, and those whose cumulative experience of criticism of themselves and their work has led them to respond with rejection of what is offered by schools. They share common feelings of resentment, frustration and aggression, which, if allowed expression in the classroom, make teaching very difficult and the learning context for other pupils very much impoverished. Those children who, by contrast, develop skill in reading and writing are reinforced in their learning as success meets with both approval and further success. They support the aims of schools, and some of them enrich schooling with their personal resources and with the resources they tap in the home and world outside school. But, after our discussion in this chapter, we may ask whether even for these children education has been all it might have been. We have brought out even more fully the implications of examining the place of language in education, and we are reminded of Stenhouse's (1967) comment that children may often have learned to read, but not been enabled to enter into the spirit of humane letters.

7

Handicaps and Hazards

The introduction to this book implied that educational attainment is related to a complex of language skills and knowledge in which the kind of socio-linguistic differences described by Deutsch and Bernstein played but a part. The elaboration of this theme has led to a fairly detailed consideration of the language skills of both teachers and pupils in various educational activities. Points at which handicap or misunderstanding might occur proved to be many and varied, but simple determining relations between language and attainment proved elusive.

The second chapter dealt with the nature of language skill in schoolchildren and with the nature of language learning. A principal conclusion to this section was that in a very important sense language as a symbolic system is itself a construction of knowledge, built by the individual within the conventions of his cultural and social context. Within the constraints of interpersonal agreement linguistic knowledge can be said to be shared, but the individual thinker utilises his own constructions in his own way to make his own version of what is intelligible. It was shown how all children face intellectual problems in acquiring language, how they encounter new forms, grasp their functions and their relationships with others, and judge when and how to use them. It is clearly not the case that language is somehow developed as an additional system to other forms of knowledge but that, given the social and intellectual characteristics of man, it is an essential part of human nature. Those who are deprived of aspects of language skill are rightly felt to be handicapped as persons, whether their disability lies within themselves or rests in physical or social isolation. This is not to see them as lesser persons or as incapable of sensible and logical thinking, but it is to appreciate that, as the blind man finds unusual ways of perceiving to cope with his blindness, so the person with a language disability finds other ways of representing and guiding his thinking and of attempting to formulate and share his thoughts. Language acquisition, for most children, *is* learning, not a condition of learning; and external guidance of this learning is the informal education he receives in his family and from the broader context of his life. Deliberate external guidance is the business of formal education and it requires, as a minimal condition of success, some grasp on the part of the tutor of the intellectual problems faced by the learner in extending his knowledge of the language of what is to be learned. Mind must reach out to mind to know what is to be known, and this cannot normally be done without groping and clarification through verbal exchange. The big danger is that verbal expressions may be taken for granted as though knowledge were contained in them, rather than worked over and reconstructed towards truer insight.

From differences in language skills amongst pupils due to factors of age and intellect, the discussion moved to those of the contexts of language learning. Here the Bernstein thesis was examined in some detail and the nature of deprivation and difference in language experience was explored. It was concluded that, although different kinds of deprivation of experience of the world and of language can be described, there is no hard evidence for the effects of social-class-based socio-linguistic code differences on educational attainment or, indeed, for their reality in any serious sense. Nevertheless the whole complex of living conditions, ways of life, parental values and expectations in a child's upbringing is likely to affect his ways of talking and his responses to others. Although the existence of well-defined subcultural groups with associated socio-linguistic codes was questioned, substantial differences in the life styles and language abilities of children were recognised. These could be attributed in part to social background variation but major differences between children within social groups were noted. Children entering school bring varied language skills and expectations about language use in different contexts. Which of these affect educational attainment is likely to rest in part on how teachers interpret and act upon the differences. As they stand, class and dialect language differences may not be of a kind to be particularly relevant to the tasks of schooling and children may, given appropriate treatment, prove as adaptable to the variants of language in school as they do to those outside. While it is evident that dialect and code differences may sometimes prove difficult for the children, it is also true that teachers' responses to differences are far from uniform. As it could not be concluded that Bernstein had made a case for claiming a direct relationship between socio-linguistic codes and educational attainment, his further argument that it is effected through aspects of autonomy and control could not be sustained—the more so since it could be doubted whether the social control in most primary schools bears a particularly strong similarity to middle-class family life!

Deprivation was interpreted as a lack of experience, either of the world about or of the language related to it, which led not so much to language differences in usage, but to impoverishment of the means of talking—to a relative lack of vocabulary and to a more limited syntax. Again some correlation wth social class is found, but again the individual home is the centre of what does or does not go on. It was recognised that immigrant children have special and particular language difficulties, but it was also recognised that some children take much longer than their age-mates to master the same vocabulary and syntax, and that this developmental lag is more apparent in lower working-class homes. There are, therefore, linguistic differences other than those of socio-linguistic code to affect the pupils' learning. These may well incline educators to seek compensatory measures, but, as the discussion of teaching young children showed particularly well, the problem of mutual understanding between teacher and child raises far more questions than those of planning a programme. And however successful compensatory pre-school education might prove to be (and there is grave doubt about the measures tried so far) the problem of background deprivation is likely to remain with children throughout their school lives. This seriously affects not only their use of spoken language but also their access to reading and to subject specialisms. In the time these children spend in school, is it possible that more might be done for them?

The discussion of using language for learning in chapters 4 and 5 drew not only on ways of approaching the place of verbal instruction in teaching but also on the general classroom contexts of learning and on specific features of verbal guidance. This analysis indicated that language was related to educational disadvantage in yet further ways. Methods of instruction involve verbal communication and guidance in different ways and to different extents. Decisions made by teachers as to how to go about guiding learning may not always lead to methods which provide understanding by pupils. Insight and learning may fail to occur not because the pupil lacks linguistic abilities but because the mode of guiding instruction fails to get necessary messages across. It was argued that differences in interest and achievement amongst pupils attributable to language problems would relate in part to the ways teachers worked. Further, how teachers react to the language and associated expectations of pupils, how they use language to frame the social status and roles of teacher and learner, and how they control pupil behaviour in the classroom create the contexts in which pupils thrive or find frustration and rejection. Moreover, the behaviour, the manner of speaking, and the linguistic options taken up by pupils profoundly affect both the general course of lessons and the specific behaviour of individuals. It was suggested that a socio-linguistic analysis of classroom codes within schools might be at least as important as the more general analysis of codes within the wider society. Socio-linguistic variation as seen by Bernstein might be not so much a causal factor in educational variation as a pointer to ways the latter might be analysed. It was virtually argued that educational cultures yield educational-linguistic codes that in turn yield differences in taking up 'educational knowledge'.

The development of educational cultures is obviously no easy matter to explore, but in looking at functions of language in education we have come to define dimensions which seem to bear analysis. School life is set in the measure of curriculum decision as given to the teacher by various authority figures outside the classroom. Different knowledge may be judged appropriate for different pupils at the level of government reports and legislation as well as at the advisory levels of educational writers, curriculum developers and local authority services. Further decisions might be made in the working out of local provision of schooling and the allocation of resources to schools. Often these judgements are made with reference to generalisations about pupils' oral and written language abilities and interests; but they should be open to critical assessment. In this connection the work of Byrne and Williamson (1975) in analysing the determinants of educational attainment has shown that the possibility of local authority provision contributing to the formation of different educational cultures is a real one.

But, external influences apart, there is a considerable responsibility for curriculum decision resting on the shoulders of head and class teachers. In looking at the question of language and the curriculum in schools, the discussion in chapters 4 and 5 rested on the definition of knowledge to be acquired that was developed in the first chapter. It differed from the implied definition in the Hadow Report (1931): 'The curriculum is to be thought of in terms of activity and experience rather than knowledge to be acquired and facts to be stored.' Plowden (1967) interpreted the intended meaning in the quotation to be that activity and experience were the means of gaining knowledge, but this seems to be to regard knowledge as a fixed outcome, whereas the view expressed in this book regards it as subject to continual appraisal and modification. We have thought of the curriculum as the selection and management of the acquiring of knowledge, and of knowledge as a plastic mental state involving personal constructions in mental and physical activity and experience which are guided in some measure by a teacher. Activities take place in recognisable episodes with beginnings and ends, but knowledge rests in understanding which always has gaps and open ends and is continually negotiated. When questions of the activities and experiences of children in school were explored, the possibilities of different curricula contributing to the emergence of educational subcultures were seriously considered. The likely outcomes of various ways of dealing with pupils' different abilities were also touched upon. In all it seemed that whatever direct effects such selections of curricula or pupils might have, the modes of verbal exchange that could develop between teachers and pupils as a result of their perceptions of each other could also play a powerful part. Certain curriculum decisions and selection procedures could result in classroom contexts more conducive to one kind of dialogue than another, but might not themselves be the major determinants. Various ways of talking in defining roles, discipline and attitudes, and in expressing values placed on discussion and literacy, were thought to play a major part in contributing to the formation of educational subcultures.

A further dimension to that of the nature of the curriculum as determined within the school is that of the home-school transition, not just on school entry, but throughout school life. All children live in two cultures—home life is their experience of whatever social subculture their parents lean towards, while school life is their sampling of an educational subculture. But by virtue of being within different neighbourhoods, the social membership of schools reflects to some extent the social subcultures of the wider society. Thus the values and norms of home influence those of school, and a school may, under the umbrella of the values and ways held and expected by the teachers, harbour different subcultures amongst the pupils. While ways of using language, and levels of skill in its use, may vary in the wider social scene, it is within school that the link with educational attainment is forged; for it is there that pupils actually become involved to a greater or lesser extent in various aspects of the curriculum. Insofar as the use of language is concerned it has been suggested that social differences do not necessarily command different curricula, that indeed the latter may be more divisive than different responses to a common curriculum. Nevertheless, pupils' readiness to take up what is offered in schooling may relate to more fundamental differences than those of language, namely to different views of the world that might well be termed different constructions of knowledge. It is beyond the scope of this book to discuss this question—a question raised by Berger and Luckman (1966). It raises problems not easily dismissed, but insofar as we have claimed that to learn to use language *is* to construct knowledge we are constrained to say that, whatever differences may lie in subcultural views of the world, the extent to which a common language is shared is a measure of the possibility of shared understanding within the larger society, both at the level of 'everyday knowledge' and at that of scholarly and scientific knowledge. Indeed, for many people—and not only from academic or middle-class circles—there are no clear boundaries between the two. If pupils come to exclude themselves from schooling, or if schools come to deprive them of access to knowledge that they could at least begin to share, then the matter is not simply one of different cultural needs and expectations but is rather a more serious question—that of the breakdown of social cohesion through deliberate action. It is a political matter. Through the language of 'subject' matter and through the medium of literacy power is exercised that has implications for both the individual and society. Access to and mastery of these forms of language gives access to positions of control in social affairs and encourages recourse to considered discussion and rationality (though obviously not guaranteeing them); while rejection of these forms leaves a man with little to use save his physical skills and physical aggression, and precious little to protect him from irrationality and exploitation save his native wit.

What curriculum decisions and home-school dimensions contribute to the formation of educational subcultures depends on the working out of classroom behaviour in ways that were explored in chapter 5. The power politics of the classroom set the scene for learning, and they find expression and are exercised in particular uses of language. Pupil power is worked out through the dynamics of personal interaction within and between the cliques they create, while teacher power is exercised in the language of control of the learning context and of the process of teaching. Pupils' cliques reflect previous educational attainment, expectations for the future, attitudes towards teachers and what is to be taught, and attitudes towards ways of living as expressed in the home. Pupil and teacher power can so interact as to profoundly affect individual children's learning. Sometimes the effect of support or rejection in this interaction will outweigh factors such as intelligence, home support and aspirations, and the support or rejection is expressed in the speech of pupils and teachers.

If the discussion in this book has at times seemed very critical of teachers, let it be said now that in any ideal sense their job is impossible. Parental responsibility itself has no end, and the phrase *in loco parentis* cannot be interpreted literally, except very narrowly to imply responsibility similar to a parent's for a child's physical safety. In no sense can a teacher achieve the measure of interaction of parent with child—even allowing that the latter may go wildly astray. In any sense of bringing up the child to develop the chosen skills and hold the cherished values of the parent, then the term can only be applied to tutors carefully chosen by parents to stand in for them in a one-to-one personal relationship. No teacher in school can be asked or expected to do this; the number of pupils in the class, the variety of parental values and interests, and the variety of teachers encountered by the pupils make it impossible. Perhaps the nearest to private tutoring is found in some independent schooling and in those snippets of the state sector where parents can choose and are lucky enough to find the kind of teaching they want for their children. The educational reality for most children is that, irrespective of differences between them, they simply face what teaching is provided when it comes; and the question of responsibility for that provision is left obscure. If teachers are not acting in place of, or on behalf of, parents, to whom are they responsible and for what? At present, as we have seen in our discussions, many teachers are perplexed—and with good reason. They face the daily task of teaching, caught between problems on all fronts. If it is to mean anything to them they have to seek to understand what they are trying to do, both in wider social terms and in terms of the culture and language of their own school. They have to try to understand not only the purpose of their teaching, but also the place of what they teach in the spectrum of human knowledge. In these matters are they to work out their own insights, singly or together, or are they to seek guidance from elsewhere, to be followed without too much worry? If the latter, are they not becoming living denials of the very educational ideals they often hold dear? If the former, are they not being asked to bear a very heavy burden without sufficient support? For as they seek their insights they also face the infinitely demanding task of trying to understand the talking and thinking, the values and behaviours of many, many children. It is surely no criticism of teachers to use illustrations of their difficulties to point out that sometimes the totality of what is being asked of them is not humanly possible, and that, unless their difficulties are met, our educational system is selling our children short.

Short measure in education is often thought of in terms of poor attainment compared with some expected norm. But from the viewpoint of the place of language in learning and teaching much more than years of schooling or examination success is involved. To sell a child short is to fail to give it the chance to learn what it can with someone who knows how to help. It is to limit the learning of any child, even those who seem to have most success. And it is to produce a situation where failure in communication forces a child to defend himself rather than to venture to break new ground. John Holt (1969) has sensitively described some of the conditions of failure in this sense, giving us pictures of children who spend their time finding ways to avoid learning and its consequent personal risk. He indicated two major consequences of breakdown in the teacher-learner dialogue: that the child might simply attempt to do what the teacher seems to ask without understanding the real requirement, and that he might feel so much at sea and under attack that he can do nothing but defend himself. In the first case strategies like watching for the cues the teacher unwittingly gives towards correct answers can pay off handsomely. Teachers often set their lips or turn their bodies or prepare to make some blackboard mark in anticipation of confirming a correct answer from a pupil, so that the likely best move can fairly readily be seen. A further strategy is simply to give up trying to understand, and just learn 'by heart'. Holt's example of Emily's tactics for defending herself is a clear illustration of what a child who feels lost and attacked tries to do. This child could not bear to be wrong and was so fearful of the possibility that she could scarcely learn. She tried to hide herself by raising her hand to questions whether she knew the answer or not, hoping that the teacher would then turn to someone else; but she could only do this if enough hands were raised to reduce the awful possibility that she might be asked even so. When she could not avoid an answer she mumbled it, knowing that there was quite a chance that the teacher would interpret the mumble as the right answer and would 'repeat it'. We could add further to this list of illustrations, and so could most teachers; but our main point is that to label the actions as those of a dull or inhibited child would be to miss the point that the dullness and inhibition can be learned responses when adequate communication in teaching and learning breaks down, when language in its broadest sense is being used in misleading ways.

More serious effects of dialogue breakdown are suggested by Seligman (1975), whose analysis of learning indicates that chronic and paralysing states of helplessness can be learned. Repeated situations in which one's actions seem to have no reliable or consistent effect can induce in a person such a profound sense of helplessness that all the characteristic signs of severe depression are shown. If desired learning is to depend on appropriate guidance and adequate feedback information, then it will not take place under conditions of seemingly random signs—the learner is utterly lost. Seligman gives instances of experimental work that show how even a temporary experience of such a state affects learning. When a group of kindergarten children was given a series of manageable and rewarded tasks while another had no such tasks and a third was randomly rewarded whether tasks were solved or not, the last group was by far the slowest to manage another set of similar problems. The children in it had no sense of mastery or direction in what they were doing. Another instance showed that older children could solve problems with one teacher but failed to solve identical problems with another teacher who had previously given them unsolvable work. Seligman considers the observations to be relevant to everyday classroom experience, and particularly to the state of mind of pupils who show severe learning blocks. He quotes examples of how some such pupils have been helped to unlearn their helplessness and to develop a new sense of control and competence. In particular he gives examples in the familiar areas of 'freezing' in reading and arithmetic skills.

Though we may all learn to feel helpless in some measure at some time or other, the weight of an overwhelming experience of persistent helplessness can scarcely be conducive to the full personal development of the sufferer. We are here moving explicitly into the field of mental well-being, bringing out what has been implicit throughout this book, namely that in all learning, even the most cognitively abstract, the person is fully involved and is involved with other persons. Either new experience is constructively integrated in the previous self or it is taken up in a distorted or meaningless way. Those techniques of managing behaviour which emphasise a one-way control system—and they are evident in many classroom contexts—are also seen in certain psychiatric practices when the patient's self-control is judged to be in doubt. But in many psychiatric approaches to treatment the patient's control of his own ways of seeing matters is seen to be crucial, and techniques which encourage reflection, or the mutual testing out of thoughts and emotions in dialogue which is a real two-way communication system, are encouraged. Where the relative values of control and reflection are clearly an issue in the treatment of certain kinds of personal limitation and mental suffering, then it is possible that their place in personal development in educational settings is more important than is generally recognised. Without wishing to confuse education with treatment of some diagnosed disorder, it would seem to be safe to say that if early learning has been distorted then the possibility of re-learning is worth considering, and if present learning is also subject to possible distortion then some evaluation of ways of avoiding it is worthwhile.

The analysis of the role of language in teaching and learning that we have attempted in this book suggests that avoidance of distorted learning and the promotion of constructive learning might be helped by attending to the development of adequate communication between pupil and teacher. The essence of the language that might be used is that it expresses care and consideration, that it promotes agreement and understanding, that it opens the minds of both teacher and taught, that it honours what is judged to be good in the life and achievements of mankind, and that it remains open to rationality. These considerations point to the grave dangers in translating the current plea for a language policy across the curriculum as a call simply to make children better speakers and better readers in some normative technical sense. But it also allows vision of where pitfalls in education may lie and of what sort of questions must be faced in considering the task of how to go about educating children in a complex society. In fostering humanity we might do worse than be guided in part by the thinking of Martin Buber (1947) who saw education as a selection of the effective world for man or child, and educating as a dialogue, in its fullest sense, between teacher and taught.

References

Adelman, C. (1973), 'Informal talk—informal education' (paper presented in the University of Leeds, based on work for the Ford Teaching Project).

Argyle, M. (1969), *Social Interaction* (London, Methuen).

Ausubel, D. P. (1961), 'In defense of verbal learning', *Educational Theory*, 11, pp. 15-25.

Bambridge, G. de P. (1975), 'Metaphor (and simile) used by children', *Cambridge Journal of Education*, 5, pp. 118-24.

Banks, O. and Finlayson, D. (1973), *Success and Failure in the Secondary School* (London, Methuen).

Bantock, G. H. (1968), *Culture, Industrialisation and Education* (London, Routledge & Kegan Paul).

Bantock, G. H. (1971), 'Towards a theory of popular education', in R. Hooper (ed.), *The Curriculum: Context, Design and Development* (Edinburgh, Oliver & Boyd).

Barnes, D. (1969), 'Language in the secondary classroom', in D. Barnes, J. Britton and H. Rosen (eds), *Language, the Learner and the School* (Harmondsworth, Penguin).

Barnes, D. (1976), *From Communication to Curriculum* (Harmondsworth, Penguin).

Bellack, A. A. *et al.* (1966), *The Language of the Classroom* (New York, Teachers College Press).

Bereiter, C. and Engelmann, S. (1966), *Teaching Disadvantaged Children in the Pre-school* (New Jersey, Prentice-Hall, Inc).

Bernstein, B. (1960), 'Language and social class', *British Journal of Sociology*, 11, pp. 271-6.

Bernstein, B. (1962), 'Linguistic codes, hesitation phenomena and intelligence', *Language and Speech*, 5, pp. 31-46.

Bernstein, B. (1971), 'Social class, language and socialisation', in B. Bernstein (ed.), *Class Codes and Control* (London, Routledge & Kegan Paul).

Bernstein, B. and Brandis, W. (1970), 'Social class differences in communication and control', in W. Brandis and D. Henderson (eds), *Social Class, Language and Communication* (London, Routledge & Kegan Paul).

Bernstein, B. and Henderson, D. (1969), 'Social class differences in the relevance of language to socialisation', *Sociology*, 3, pp. 1-20.

Blank, M. (1973), Appendix to M. H. Moss (ed.), *Deprivation and Disadvantage. E262 Block 8* (Bletchley, Open University Press).

Blank, M. and Solomon, F. (1968), 'A tutorial language program to develop abstract thinking in socially disadvantaged preschool children', *Child Development*, 39, pp. 379-89.

Britton, J. (1969), 'Talking to learn', in D. Barnes, J. Britton and H. Rosen (eds), *Language, the Learner and the School* (Harmondsworth, Penguin).

Britton, J. (1970), *Language and Learning* (Harmondsworth, Penguin).

Brown, R. (1973), *A First Language: The Early Stages* (Cambridge, Mass., Harvard University Press).

Bruner, J. S. (1959), 'Learning and thinking', *Harvard Educational Review*, 29, pp. 184-92.

Bruner, J. S. (1960), *The Process of Education* (Cambridge, Mass., Harvard University Press).

Bruner, J. S. (1961), 'The act of discovery', *Harvard Educational Review*, 31, pp. 21-32.

Bruner, J. S. (1966), 'On the conservation of liquids', in J. S. Bruner *et al.* (eds.), *Studies in Cognitive Growth* (New York, Wiley).

Bryant, P. (1974), *Perception and Understanding in Young Children* (London, Methuen).

132 *Language in Teaching and Learning*

Buber, M. (1947), *Between Man and Man. III. Education* (London, Kegan Paul).
Bullock, A. (1975), *A Language for Life*, Report of the Committee of Inquiry appointed by the Secretary of State for Education and Science (London, HMSO).
Burt, C. (1937), *The Backward Child* (London, University of London Press).
Byrne, D. S., Williamson, W. and Fletcher, J. (1975), *The Poverty of Education* (London, Robertson).
Cazden, C. (1972) *Child Language and Education* (New York, Holt, Rinehart & Winston).
Chomsky, C. (1969), *The Acquisition of Syntax in Children from 5-10* (Cambridge, Mass., MIT Press).
Clarke, E. V. (1971), 'On the acquisition of the meaning of *before* and *after*', *Journal of Verbal Learning and Verbal Behavior*, 10, pp. 266-75.
Clark, E. V. (1973), 'Non-linguistic strategies and the acquisition of word meanings', *Cognition*, 2, pp. 161-82.
Clark, E. V. and Garnica, O. K. (1974), 'Is he coming or going? On the acquisition of deictic verbs', *Papers and Reports on Child Language Development* (Committee on Linguistics, Stanford University), 7, pp. 1-23.
Clark, M. M. (1975), 'Language and reading—a study of early reading', in W. Latham (ed.), *The Road to Effective Reading* (London, Ward Lock).
Cook-Gumperz, J. (1973), *Social Control and Socialisation* (London, Routledge & Kegan Paul).
Creber, J. W. P. (1972), *Lost for Words* (Harmondsworth, Penguin).
Davie, R., Butler, N. and Goldstein, H., (1972), *From Birth to Seven* (London, Longman).
Dearden, R. F. (1967), 'Instruction and learning by discovery', in R. S. Peters (ed.), *The Concept of Education* (London, Routledge & Kegan Paul.
Deutsch, M. (ed.), (1967), *The Disadvantaged Child* (New York, Basic Books).
Doman, G. (1964), *How to Teach your Baby to Read* (New York, Random House).
Donaldson, M. and Balfour, G. (1968), 'Less is more : a study of language comprehension in children', *British Journal of Psychology*, 59, pp. 461-71.
Donaldson, M. and McGarrigle, J. (1974), 'Some clues to the nature of semantic development', *Journal of Child Language*, 1, pp. 185-94.
Douglas, J. W. B. (1964), *The Home and the School* (London, McGibbon & Kee).
Douglas, J. W. B. (1968), *All our Future* (London, Peter Davies).
Downing, J. (1970), 'Children's concepts of language in learning to read', *Educational Research*, 9, pp. 56-62.
Edwards, A. D. (1976), *Language in Culture and Class* (London, Heinemann).
Ervin-Tripp, S. (1971), 'An overview of theories of grammatical development', in D. I. Slobin (ed.), *The Ontogenesis of Grammar* (New York, Academic Press).
Ferguson, C. A. (1959), 'Diglossia', *Word*, 15, pp. 325-40.
Fishman, J. A. (1965), 'Who speaks what language to whom and when', *La Linguistique*, 2, pp. 67-88.
Flanders, N. A. (1970), *Analyzing Teaching Behavior* (New York, Addison-Wesley).
Flude, M. (1974), 'Sociological accounts of different educational attainment', in M. Flude and J. Ahier (eds), *Educability, Schools and Ideology* (London, Croom Helm).
Francis, H. (1972), 'Towards an explanation of the syntagmatic-paradigmatic shift', *Child Development*, 43, pp. 949-58.
Francis, H. (1973), 'Children's experience of reading and notions of units in language', *British Journal of Educational Psychology*, 43, pp. 17-23.
Francis, H. (1974a), 'Social class, reference and context', *Language and Speech*, 17, pp. 193-8.
Francis, H. (1974b), 'Social background, speech and learning to read', *British Journal of Educational Psychology*, 44, pp. 290-9.
Francis, H. (1975), *Language in Childhood* (London, Elek Press).
Francis, P. (1975), *Beyond Control?* (London, Allen & Unwin).

Furth, H. G. (1966), *Thinking without Language : Psychological Implications of Deafness* (London, Collier-Macmillan).

Gage, N. L. (1967), 'Psychological conceptions of teaching', *International Journal of Educational Science*, 1, pp. 151-61.

Gagne, R. M. and Smith, E. C. (1962), 'A study of the effects of verablisation on problem-solving', *Journal of Experimental Psychology*, 63, pp. 12-18.

Gillard, H. C. (1975), 'Factors affecting the efficient reading of science text-books—a pilot study', in W. Latham (ed.), *The Road to Effective Reading* (London, Ward Lock).

Goffman, E. (1959), *The Presentation of Self in Everyday Life* (Harmondsworth, Penguin).

Gregory, S. (1973), 'Learning to discriminate—the learning of meanings' paper presented at the British Psychological Society Developmental Section Conference, September 1973).

Guillaume, P. (1926), *L'Imitation Chez L'Enfant* (translated version: *Imitation in Children*, 1971, Chicago, University of Chicago Press).

Hadow Report (1931), *Report of the Consultative Committee on the Primary School* (London, HMSO).

Halliday, M. A. K. (1973), *Explorations in the Functions of Language* (London, Arnold).

Halsey, A. H. (1972), *Educational Priority, vol. 1, EPA Problems and Policies* (London, HMSO).

Harding, A. (1975), 'Social class, task requirements and children's speech'. Dissertation submitted in part-requirement for the degree of M.Ed., Department of Education, University of Leeds).

Hargreaves, D. H. (1967), *Social Relations in a Secondary School* (London, Routledge & Kegan Paul).

Haviland, S. E. and Clark, E. V. (1973), 'This man's father is my father's son. A study of the acquisition of English kin terms', *Papers and Reports on Child Language Development* (Committee on Linguistics, Stanford University), 5, pp. 1-30.

Hawkins, P. R. (1969), 'Social class, the nominal group and reference', *Language and Speech*, 12, pp. 25-35.

Hayes, E. J. (1975), 'The reading habits and interests of adolescents and adults', in W. Latham (ed.), *The Road to Effective Reading* (London, Ward Lock).

Henderson, D. (1970a), 'Social class differences in form class usage among five-year-old children', in W. Brandis and D. Henderson (eds), *Social Class, Language and Communication* (London, Routledge & Kegan Paul).

Henderson, D. (1970b), 'Contextual specificity, discretion and cognitive specialisation: with special reference to language', *Sociology*, 4, pp. 311-37.

Hess, R. D. and Shipman, V. C. (1965), 'Early experience and the socialisation of cognitive modes in children', *Child Development*, 36, pp. 869-86.

Hirst, P. (1974), *Knowledge and the Curriculum* (London, Routledge & Kegan Paul).

Holding, D. H. (1965), *Principles of Training* (Oxford, Pergamon).

Holt, J. (1969), *How Children Fail* (Harmondsworth, Penguin).

Holt, J. (1971), *The Underachieving School* (Harmondsworth, Penguin).

Inhelder, B. *et al.* (1974), *Learning and the Development of Cognition* (London, Routledge & Kegan Paul).

Isaacs, S. (1930), *Intellectual Growth in Young Children* (London, Routledge).

Johnson-Laird, P. N. *et al.* (1972), 'Reasoning and a sense of reality', *British Journal of Psychology*, 63, pp. 395-400.

Jones, R. M. (1966), 'Education in Depth' and 'The New Curricula', in R. M. Jones (ed.), *Contemporary Educational Psychology* (New York, Harper & Row).

Jones, R. M. (1968), *Fantasy and Feeling in Education* (New York, University Press).

Keddie, N. (1971), 'Classroom knowledge', in M. F. D. Young (ed.), *Knowledge and Control* (London, Collier-Macmillan).

Kohl, H. (1975), *Reading, How to* (Harmondsworth, Penguin).

Kounin, J. S. (1970), *Discipline and Group Management in Classrooms* (New York, Holt, Rinehart & Winston).

Kuenne, M. R. (1946), 'Experimental investigation of the relation of language to transposition behavior in young children', *Journal of Experimental Psychology*, 36, pp. 471-90.

Kuhn, T. S. (1970), *The Structure of Scientific Revolutions* (Chicago, University of Chicago Press).

Labov, W. (1969), 'The logic of nonstandard English', *Georgetown Monographs on Language and Linguistics*, 22, pp. 1-31; also in P. P. Giglioli (ed.), *Language and Social Context* (Harmondsworth, Penguin).

Lacey, C. (1970), *Hightown Grammar : The School as a Social System* (Manchester, Manchester University Press).

Lawton, D. (1968), *Social Class, Language and Education* (London, Routledge & Kegan Paul).

Lawton, D. (1975), *Class, Culture and the Curriculum* (London, Routledge & Kegan Paul).

Lippman, M. Z. (1971), 'Correlates of contrast word associations: developmental trends', *Journal of Verbal Learning and Verbal Behavior*, 10, pp. 392-9.

Loban, W. D. (1963), *The Language of Elementary School Children* (Research Report No. 1, National Council of Teachers of English, Champaign, Illinois).

Lonergan, B. J. F. (1968), *Insight: A study of Human Understanding* (London, Longman).

Loughton, M. (1969), 'Child from a non-reading home', *Times Educational Supplement*, 10 October 1969.

Luria, A. R. (1959), 'The directive function of speech in development and dissolution, part 1', *Word*, 15, pp. 341-52.

Luria, A. R. (1961), *The Role of Speech in the Regulation of Normal and Abnormal Behaviour* (London, Pergamon).

Merritt, J. E. (1971), *Reading and the Curriculum* (London, Ward Lock).

Midwinter, E. (1972), *Priority Education* (Harmondsworth, Penguin).

Morris, J. M. (1966), *Standards and Progress in Reading* (Slough, NFER).

Morrison, A. and McIntyre, D. (1973), *Teachers and Teaching* (Harmondsworth, Penguin, 2nd edition).

Moseley, D. and Hamblin, D. (1972), *Intervening in the Learning Process*, Open University Course E281, Units 16 & 17 (Bletchley, Open University Press).

Moyle, D. (1975), 'Approaching reading in the middle school', in W. Latham (ed.), *The Road to Effective Reading* (London, Ward Lock).

Musgrove, F. (1968), 'The contribution of sociology to the study of the curriculum', in J. Kerr (ed.), *Changing the Curriculum* (London, University of London Press).

Nash, R. (1973), *Classrooms Observed* (London, Routledge & Kegan Paul).

Newsom Report (1963), *Half our Future. A report of the Central Advisory Council for Education to the Department of Education and Science* (London, HMSO).

Newson, J. (1974), 'Towards a theory of infant understanding', *Bulletin of the British Psychological Society*, 27, pp. 251-7.

Newson, J. and Newson, E. (1970), *Four Years Old in an Urban Community* (Harmondsworth, Penguin).

Newson, J. and Packer, S. (1973), 'Imitation and pre-verbal communication' (paper presented at the British Psychological Society Developmental Section Conference, September 1973).

Neville, M. H. and Pugh, A. K. (1974), 'Context in reading and listening: a comparison of children's errors in cloze tests', *British Journal of Educational Psychology*, 44, pp. 224-32.

O'Connor, N. and Hermelin, B. (1962), *Speech and Thought in Severe Subnormality* (London, Pergamon).

Opie, I. and Opie, P. (1959), *The Lore and Language of School-children* (Oxford, Clarendon Press).

Otty, N. (1972), *Learner Teacher* (Harmondsworth, Penguin).

Peel, E. A. (1971), *The Nature of Adolescent Judgment* (London, Staples Press).

Piaget, J. (1928), *Judgment and Reasoning in the Child* (London, Routledge & Kegan Paul).

Piaget, J. (1959), *Language and Thought of the Child* (A translation from the French 1926 edition) (London, Routledge & Kegan Paul).

Piaget, J. (1962), *Comments on Vygotsky's Critical Remarks Concerning 'The Language and Thought of the Child' and 'Judgment and Reasoning in the Child'* (Cambridge, Mass. MIT Press).

Plowden Report (1967), *Children and their Primary Schools. A report of the Central Advisory Council for Education to the Department of Education and Science* (London, HMSO).

Postman, N. (1970), 'The politics of reading', *Harvard Educational Review*, 40, pp. 244-52.

Pride, J. B. and Holmes, J. (eds), (1972), *Sociolinguistics* (Harmondsworth, Penguin).

Pugh, A. K. (1971), 'Secondary school reading: obstacles to profit and delight', *Reading*, 5, pp. 6-13.

Reid, J. F. (1966), 'Learning to think about reading', *Educational Research*, 9, pp. 56-62.

Richards, M. P. M. (1971), 'Social interaction in the first weeks of human life', *Psychiatry, Neurology and Neurochirurgery*, 74, pp. 35-42.

Riley, C. M. D. and Epps, F. M. J. (1967), *Headstart in Action* (New York, Parker).

Robinson, W. P. (1972), *Language and Social Behaviour* (Harmondsworth, Penguin).

Robinson, W. P. and Rackstraw, S. J. (1967), 'Variations in mothers' answers to children's questions', *Sociology*, 1, pp. 259-79.

Robinson, W. P. and Rackstraw, S. J. (1972), *A Question of Answers* (London, Routledge & Kegan Paul).

Rosen, C. and Rosen, H. (1973), *The Language of Primary School Children* (Harmondsworth, Penguin).

Rosen, H. (1972), 'The language of text-books', in A. Cashdan *et al.* (eds), *Language in Education* (London, Routledge & Kegan Paul).

Schaffer, H. R. (1974), 'Early social behaviour and the study of reciprocity', *Bulletin of the British Psychological Society*, 27, pp. 211-12.

Seligman, C. R. *et al.* (1970), 'The effects of speech style on teachers' attitudes towards pupils', (unpublished manuscript, McGill University, Montreal).

Seligman, M. (1975), *Helplessness* (San Francisco, Freeman).

Shields, M. M. and Steiner, E. (1973), 'The language of three to five-year-olds in pre-school education', *Educational Research*, 15, pp. 97-105.

Sinclair, J. McH. and Coulthard, M. (1975), *Towards an Analysis of Discourse* (Oxford, Oxford University Press).

Sinclair-de Zwart, H. (1967), *Acquisition du Langage et Développement de la Pensée* (Paris, Dunod).

Slobin, D. (1966), 'The acquistion of Russian as a native language', in F. Smith and G.A. Miller (eds), *The Genesis of Language* (Cambridge, Mass., MIT Press).

Smith, B. O. and Meux, M. O. (1970), *A Study of the Logic of Teaching* (Urbana, University of Illinois Press).

Soderbergh, R. (1971), *Reading in Early Childhood* (Stockholm, Almqvist & Wiksell).

Southgate, V. (1966), 'A few comments on "Reading Drive",' *Educational Research*, 9, pp. 145-6.

Sprott, W. J. H. (1958), *Human Groups* (Harmondsworth, Penguin).

Stenhouse, L. (1967), *Culture and Education* (London, Nelson).

Stenhouse, L. (1975), *An Introduction to Curriculum Research and Development* (London, Heinemann).

Stones, E. (1970), 'Verbal labelling and concept formation in primary school children', *British Journal of Educational Psychology*, 40, pp. 245-52.

Strickland, R. G. (1962), 'The language of elementary school children; its relationship to the language of reading textbooks and the quality of reading in selected children', *Bulletin of the School of Education, Indiana University*, 38.

Templin, M. C. (1957), *Certain Language Skills in Children* (Minneapolis, University of Minnesota Press).

Torrey, J. W. (1973), 'Learning to read without a teacher: a case study', in F. Smith (ed.), *Psycholinguistics and Reading* (New York, Holt, Rinehart & Winston).

Turner, G. J. (1973), 'Social class and children's language control at ages five and seven', in B. Bernstein (ed.), *Class, Codes and Control* (London, Routledge & Kegan Paul), vol. 2.

Vygotsky, L. S. (1962), *Thought and Language* (Cambridge, Mass., MIT Press).

Walker, R. and Adelman, C. (1975), *A Guide to Classroom Observation* (London, Methuen).

Wason, P. C. (1969), 'Regression in reasoning?', *British Journal of Psychology*, 60, pp. 471-80.

Watts, A. F. (1944), *The Language and Mental Development of Children* (London, Harrap).

Whitehead, F., Capey, A. C. and Maddren, W. (1975), 'Children's reading interests', *Schools Council Working Paper 52* (London, Evans/Methuen Educational).

Whorf, B. L. (1956), *Language, Thought and Reality* (Cambridge, Mass., MIT Press).

Williams, R. (1961), *The Long Revolution* (Harmondsworth, Penguin).

Wyatt, G. L. (1969), *Language Learning and Communication Disorders in Children* (New York, Free Press).

Young, M. F. D. (1971), 'Curricula as socially organised knowledge', in M. F. D. Young (ed.), *Knowledge and Control* (London, Collier-Macmillan).

Index

abstract concepts 25, 35, 47
abstraction 23-4, 107
active speech 24
adolescent language development 36-7
adolescent thinking 36, 65
alienation 21-2, 81, 110
analogy 37
anti-school culture 81, 110, 120
Argyle 19
attainment : and language 13, 123, 126; and social class 13, 42; and socio-linguistic codes 123
attention 41
Ausubel 35, 68
avid readers 111
avoidance strategies 91-3, 114, 117, 128

backwardness in reading 103
Bambridge 37
Banks and Finlayson 21
Bantock 119
Barnes 97-8, 100-1, 116
Bellack 98
Bereiter and Engelman 43, 84
Berger and Luckman 126
Bernstein 13, 44-7, 117, 119, 122-3
Bernstein and Brandis 50
Bernstein and Henderson 50, 78
Blank 84-6
Britton 23, 31, 100
Brown 23
Bruner 23, 64-6, 68
Bryant 67
Buber 130
Byrne and Williamson 125

Cazden 52
Chomsky, C. 33
Clark, E. 29
Clark and Garnica 30
Clark, M. 104
classroom language 124; address 21, 78-82; complexity 89-91; control 21, 80, 83, 92-4, 99; interpersonal relations 78-84; nursery 84-6; primary 87-91; secondary 91-101
code-switching 46-8, 102
cognitive basis of language development 40
common curriculum 74, 119

communication failure 22, 128-30
compensatory education 43, 73, 124
compliance 91
comprehension 29-34
concept attainment 25, 34-7, 47, 62, 94-9
concrete concepts 25, 35, 47
conformity 85
conservation 64
construction of knowledge 16-18, 126
Cook-Gumperz 50, 52
Cook's tour 98
Creber 43
cross-cultural differences 72-3

Davie 13
Dearden 68
deficit 13, 43, 73-4
deprivation 13, 43, 118, 123
Deutsch 13, 43, 53, 117, 122
dialect 53-4
dialogue 16, 51, 56-9, 88-9, 130
discovery learning 67-8
displaced speech 23-4
Doman 104
Donaldson and Balfour 29
Donaldson and McGarrigle 30
Douglas 13
Downing 108

early readers 104
Edwards 42
educational-linguistic codes 102, 124
educational sub-cultures 81, 110, 121, 126
egocentrism 63, 88
elaborated code 45
encoding 61-2, 66
error 26
Ervin-Tripp 51

feedback 15, 101
Ferguson 38
fiction 110
Fishman 102
Flanders 91
Flude 42
fluency 48
focusing 98
formal code 45
formal groups 21, 81

Packer 57

parental guidance 51-3, 56-60, 104-5, 112, 115

participant function 31

Peel 36

perseverance 105

Piaget 30, 36, 63, 88, 89

Plowden Report 13, 125

'polar' pairs 28-30

Postman 118, 120

practice 105

predictability 47

presentation of facts 97

Pride and Holmes 19

primary school language development 26-35

private reading 112

problem-solving 62, 69

programmed instruction 85, 91

project work 114

psychoanalytic influence 76

public code 45

Pugh 112

pupil power 20, 91-4, 127

pupil talk 97

readiness to learn 70-1

reading : drive 104, 108; drop-out 111; interests 111; pre-school 104; primary school 104-8; middle school 110-15; secondary school 116-21; standards 103 technical vocabulary 107

reflection on speech 23-4, 31

reluctant learners 21, 81, 91, 110, 128

register 38, 98, 116

Reid 107

restricted code 45

Richards 51

Riley 13

Robinson 54

Robinson and Rackstraw 50

Rosen 116

Rosen and Rosen 87, 110

rote learning 68

Schaffer 51

school provision 112, 116, 125

secondary school language development 35-7

self guidance 61-2

Seligman 54, 129

semantic system learning 27-8

Shields and Steiner 27

Sinclair and Coulthard 98

Sinclair de Zwart 65

Slobin 29

Smith and Meux 99

social class: and attainment 13, 42; and linguistic differences 42-48, 123-4; and sub-cultures 18, 44

social reading competence 109

socialisation 50-3

sociolinguistic codes 45-50, 123

socio-linguistics 38

Soderbergh 107

Sokhin 29

Southgate 108

spectator function 31

speech: and reading 106-7; and regulation of behaviour 61-2; and thought 32-4, 46-7, 63-6

Sprott 101

Stenhouse 120, 121

stereotyping 120

Strickland 107

sub-cultural differences 13, 44, 73-4, 123

subject: concepts 94-9; reading 113, 116; register 98, 116

syntax in speech: preschool 26-7; primary school 31-4; secondary school 36-7

talking and learning 13, 100; *see also* dialogue *and* group discussion

teachers' attitudes 19, 54, 80, 82, 93-4

teacher guidance 108, 112, 114, 116

teacher talk 15, 91, 98

Templin 24, 31

text-books 108, 113, 116

thought and language 32-4, 46-7, 63-6, 84

Torrey 104, 107

Turner 50

values 18-19, 22, 52-3, 93-4, 119, 126

verbal ability 41

verbal: encoding 61-2; explanation 35; feedback 60; guidance 58-63; instruction 60-1, 68; practice 68; thought 63

vocabulary: pre-school 24; primary school 34-7; secondary school 36-7; social class 43, 44-5; subject 36, 94-9

Vygotsky 62, 63, 107

Walker and Adelman 98

Watts 33, 38

Whitehead 111

Whorf 72-3

Williams 71

writing 109, 114

Wyatt 13

Young 18, 71